Further Acclaim for *Returning to My Mother's House*

Gail Straub's new book, *Returning To My Mother's House,* is a book for mothers and daughters everywhere. Gail's thirty-year journey is a testament to the fierce power of the mother-daughter bond as a healing force in our world. This book both encourages and challenges us to take back our female wisdom, our emotional intelligence, our interior lives, our creativity and imagination, and our willingness to live with death as a wise advisor. More than anything Gail's book is a prayer that we take back this wisdom before it is too late for both our human family and our earth.

—Immaculee Ilibagiza, author of
Left to Tell: Discovering God Amidst the Rwandan Holocaust

Returning To My Mother's House is an intimately personal yet universal book. It's a rousing tale of a gutsy woman's adventures, her worldwide travels, her caring work, and her trials, tribulations, and joys. Above all, it is a daughter's tribute to her own mother, to all our mothers, and to feminine wisdom and power.

—Riane Eisler, author of
The Chalice and the Blade and *The Real Wealth of Nations*

As too many women in leadership positions know, the flame of passion and purposefulness can be extinguished by workaholism which is often rooted in a neglect of our undervalued feminine. In this biography and teaching guide, Gail Straub courageously names the undiscussable shadow aspects of achievement that have accompanied her enormous success as a global activist and beloved spiritual guide. She painfully acknowledges the legacy of her mother's lost connection to her heart's desires as a woman who extinguished her feminine voice. Gail takes us on spellbinding travels of both personal and global proportions to retrieve her own lost feminine, and reveals her own nature as an unbounded flame. Most poignantly, we as readers see Gail's bold paint strokes of vivid imagery as her mother's artistic expression finally finding its beautiful canvas. Gail leaves us with the kindling needed to fiercely yet gently examine what is required to stop, be still, and illuminate the quiet wisdom needed to lead in these urgent times.

—Ellen Wingard, Editor,
Enlightened Power: How Women Are Transforming the Practice of Leadership

Returning to My Mother's House is a sacred incantation of celestial feminine remembrance. Gail has written so tenderly, and so courageously about the crisis and opportunity that confront us all. In these tumultuous times, our mother planet is beseeching women of all ages, cultures, and dimensions to awaken, reintegrate, and honor our most precious gifts in service of ourselves and the most high. As one who has "lost" her mother at a young age, I experienced this book as an act of love, faith, and healing. It is a mantra for the reclaiming of our divine feminine purpose. I am so grateful for this deeply personal yet profoundly universal journey.

—Rha Goddess, Artist, Activist, and author of *We Got Issues*

A good book gifts its readers with an exquisite map of the human heart, and Gail Straub's *Returning to My Mother's House* does exactly that. In this healing story Gail has written an eloquent and compelling narrative of a daughter's thirty-year journey to reconnect with her late mother's authentic self, and the discovery of her own powerful feminine spirit in the process. This book addresses many questions of motherhood that spoke deeply to me: choosing to be, or not to be, a mother; looking for a mother; and finding a mother. Gail's journey takes her literally around the world but ultimately returns her to her childhood home, to the original drawer of her heart-map with the imprints of love and wisdom left there by her mother. And as her story continues Gail expands upon these imprints, and creates her own empowered map. This book honors not only Gail and her mother's spirit but also the feminine power in all of us.

—Loung Ung, author of
First They Killed My Father and *Lucky Child*

Gail Straub's memoir, *Returning to My Mother's House: Taking Back the Wisdom of the Feminine* shines as a model for a life lived outside convention. Here the remarkable Straub, who has helped thousands of people achieve their dreams with her ground-breaking Empowerment Institute, examines the dreams of her ebullient almost-artist mother, sadly unfulfilled in her shortened life. By drawing her mother's portrait in words bright with detail, Straub finds the feminine principle that she almost unwittingly sacrificed in her own life. The contrasts between the former bohemian, upward-striving mother and the international innovator daughter are both sharp and tender. As Gail Straub uncovers the forgotten layers hiding what her mother gave her, she discovers that her mother's circumscribed life prepared her for the vast changes she has been able to make in the journeys of others. In powerful and profound ways, this extraordinary woman has lived her mother's dream.

—Molly Peacock, poet, President Emerita of the Poetry Society of America, and author of *Paradise, Piece by Piece*

The journey to reclaim lost aspects of one's past and so unfold into greater wholeness is a classical and dynamic theme. In this beautifully written memoir, Gail Straub brings this process home to us in poignant and lucid ways. Her story will inspire many to look for the spiritual treasures in their own history. *Returning to My Mother's House* is an important and nourishing book.

—Gunilla Norris, author of *Inviting Silence* and *Simple Ways*

In Jungian psychology, the house is often seen as a symbol of the self. Gail Straub's return to her mother's house is the archetypal journey of the self back to the sources of its deepest wounds, as well as the sources of its deepest wisdom and healing. It is the kind of "return" that can only be made with the wisdom of time and perspective—and still it requires courage and persistence to take what Jung called "the night sea journey" into the fertile conflicts of our early houses. In her new book, *Returning to My Mother's House*, Straub bravely takes this journey for all of us—and what reader, having entered into the journey alongside this engaging soul, does not come out more whole?

—Stephen Cope, Director, Kripalu Institute
for Extraordinary Living, and author of
Yoga and the Quest for the True Self and *The Wisdom of Yoga*

Returning to My Mother's House is Gail Straub's poetic, heartfelt, and very personal journey story, but it is also my story, your story, and the story of a culture in desperate need of "taking back the wisdom of the feminine." Enough history, we need her-story! We need books like Gail's—brave tales of the feminine, lost and found. Reading this book encouraged me to go back and heal aspects of myself and my relationship with my mother. I found myself dreaming of my mother, looking at old picture albums, reading letters we wrote to each other over the years, and thinking about her—her unrealized dreams, her abandoned self, her frightened heart, and the legacy of love and loss that she passed on to me. I came away from the adventure of reading *Returning to My Mother's House* full of hope for the restoration of the feminine in each of us, and our world.

—Elizabeth Lesser, Cofounder, Omega Institute,
author of *Broken Open* and *The Seeker's Guide*

Returning to My Mother's House

Taking Back the Wisdom of the Feminine

Gail Straub

FOREWORD BY
Christiane Northrup, M.D.

2008

High Point
1649 Route 28A
West Hurley, New York 12491

10 9 8 7 6 5 4 3 2 1

First Edition

Printed in the United States of America

♾ This edition is printed on acid-free paper that meets the
American National Standards Institute z39.48 Standard.

Distributed by Chelsea Green Publishing

Design and composition: Greta D. Sibley & Associates
Author photograph: Leif Zurmuhlen
Cover photographs: Jeff DeRose/One Match Films

Cataloging Data

Straub, Gail Hyde.
Returning to my mother's house : taking back the
wisdom of the feminine /
Gail Straub; foreword by Christiane Northrup.
p. cm.
ISBN 978-0-9630327-5-1 (alk. paper)
1. Spiritual memoir.
Library of Congress Control Number: 2008924532

For My Mother
Jacqueline Walsh Straub
1917–1972

Contents

The central people in this book—my husband, family members, and close colleagues—have their real names. The names and identities of all my students have been changed and are represented as composites.

Foreword

Back in the early 1980s, it was Gail Straub's empowerment work that gave me the courage, and the inner tools, to start Women to Women, a women's medical center run by women, which was revolutionary at that time. This work became the basis for my first book, *Women's Bodies, Women's Wisdom*. Since then Gail's global activism, along with her deep spiritual inquiry, have helped thousands of others around the globe find wholeness and inspiration.

Now Gail has written her fiercely honest and personal memoir *Returning to My Mother's House: Taking Back the Wisdom of the Feminine*. As I read her book I felt like I was drinking sweet cool water after being thirsty for a long time. I drank it up, every page. There is a piece of our collective woman's story that Gail describes that I've never read anywhere else. She provided me with a piece of information that has made a tremendous difference with my own daughters. It's this: Daughters often unconsciously take on the "unlived" lives of their mothers. And this "unlived" life becomes a powerful motivating force throughout our lives. Gail helped me bring this to consciousness, thus freeing my daughters and breaking a long lineage of unconscious pain!

Gail's book describes the imprint of the feminine we each receive from our mothers; the gradual loss of both our mother's innate wisdom as well as our own; Gail's own journey that literally took her around world to find and take back her wisdom; and, finally, the commitment she ultimately made to pass on her wisdom and protect the lineage of the sacred feminine for others. Gail's story speaks to my entire generation of baby-boom women, and the way that we collectively lost our connection with the wisdom of the feminine and, often, with our own mothers. Most important, this story is about how we are finding this connection once again. Though this memoir is intensely personal, the story is universal. It's every woman's story of betraying the wisdom of our feminine and our profound longing to find it again. Because Gail's journey so clearly demonstrates that when one woman takes back her innate wisdom she does this for all the women who came before her and all the women who will come after her, all of us can find great hope for the restoration of the feminine—the source of all healing.

I am intimately familiar with the courage required to take back our female wisdom. It took me eight years to write my book *Mother-Daughter Wisdom*, a book that I really wanted to call *Mothers and Daughters: The Bond That Wounds, the Bond That Heals*. During that time, I nearly went blind in my left (feminine) eye because my process forced me to look at things I hadn't been ready to see until midlife. In order to write a book that was truly useful to women, I needed to come to grips with my own mother. Until we understand both sides of the mother-daughter bond, we can't truly reclaim our deepest feminine wisdom and power. And both Gail and I agree that this reclaiming is imperative not just for the empowerment of our daughters and grand-daughters, but also for our world.

There isn't a woman alive who won't be able to relate to this lyrical, poignant, and beautifully written story. Like Elizabeth Gilbert's *Eat, Pray, Love*, Gail's story will help women gain insight and wisdom that will not only help heal their relationships with their mothers, but could, quite frankly, help save their lives! Bless you, Gail, for doing work that heals all of us.

—Christiane Northrup, M.D.
Portland, Maine
February 2008

Every mother contains her daughter in herself and every daughter her mother, and every mother extends backwards into her mother and forwards into her daughter.

—Carl Jung

Prologue

My mother died thirty-six years ago, but the truth is she's more alive to me now than ever before. At fifty-nine I have lived four years longer than my mother did. In the these last years as I wrote about Mom, as I felt certain that I too would die at fifty-five, as my extra bonus years became a precious gift, I realized that it's impossible to separate where a mother ends and a daughter begins. I realized that those we love never really die. But what surely did die, long before my mother did, were her dreams and her connection to her innate female wisdom. A gifted and successful artist, with a passionate spirit and a wildly colorful bohemian wardrobe, my mother gradually gave up her vivid individuality as she grew into her roles as wife, working mother, and aspiring member of an upscale conservative society. Then, wrestling with a fatal illness, she died too soon. The spiritual loss, more than the physical loss of my mother, has haunted me.

This loss of my mother's authentic self has shaped my life, propelling me around the globe to reclaim what she left behind, to retrace the series of small deaths she suffered each time she abandoned more of her instinctual wisdom. I, too, betrayed my feminine, paying blind allegiance to the flag of the masculine with its bold stripes of workaholism, speed, and overdrive. Luckier than my mother, I realized that my feminine was dying before it was too late, before there was no turning back, before the spiritual dying entered my body and made me sick. With the consciousness and resources of my generation, I came to understand why I had sacrificed my interior life—the rich realm of feelings and moods, intuition and creativity, stillness and contemplation—to the overwhelming seduction of our dominant cultural values. I came to see why I had fallen under the spell of a culture that pays tribute to rational thought and exterior accomplishment, and at all costs, on all levels, encourages and rewards the principles of *bigger, more,* and *faster.*

This is the story of how I returned to my mother's house and reclaimed my own female wisdom, taking back what both Mom and I had betrayed. I see now how my story is so many of our stories. It is the story of both men and women who have abandoned their inner lives, leaving behind their hearts where deep dark feelings reside; putting aside their intuitive imagination where dreams flourish; ignoring the invisible worlds where the irrational and the mysterious offer their incomparable gifts; and disowning the realms of silence, simplicity, and solitude where the interior matures. Modern life rarely acknowledges or even allows space for such things. But we ignore these things at our peril, both as individual human beings and as an earth family.

Come, come, dear reader, return to the house of the Great Mother. Enter the soft rounded door and feel immediately welcome in the central room of the heart, fully open and exposing an enormous breadth of emotional intelligence. Sit down and rest in any of the ample cozy corners dedicated to the interior values of stillness and contemplation. Up, up, take the elegant grand staircase of relationships made up of collaboration, co-operation, communication, and caring. Only by taking these steps can you reach the upper levels of the Great Mother's house, where the rooms of intuition provide safe haven for the imagination, for dreams and symbols, for creativity and the arts. And don't forget to visit the secret dark spaces, chambers of the irrational, of death, of the wild and untamed. Take your time; these hidden spaces have much to offer. Arriving at the top of the house you find the numinous berth of the invisible, with its direct connection to the divine. I know how you feel up here in this sacred space; this is what has been missing from your life, this is what you have been so hungry for. You ache to sit here for a long time before you have to return to all that is concrete and reasonable and fast. I invite you to stay as long as you need. With all my heart I urge you to fully reinhabit this house for yourself, for your children and grandchildren, and for our earth. Do this before it is too late.

PART ONE

Living in My Mother's House

The Imprint of the Feminine

The house of my childhood is the house of
recurring dreams yet subtly altered, the rooms
mysterious, their dimensions uncertain, always
there is a promise, alarming yet tantalizing, of
rooms yet undiscovered, through a back wall,
in the attic perhaps, or the cellar, rooms to be
explored, beckoning. Your presence permeates
the house, you are the house, its mysterious
infinite rooms.

—Joyce Carol Oates,
*A Letter to My Mother Carolina Oates
on Her 78th Birthday*

My Mother the Bohemian
Unbounded Flame

White flame
On a day without wind
My love is burning
Away my mind
      —Rumi

A year after Mom died I went out to her birthplace in Denver to learn more about her life. Visiting my Aunt Mae several times over the next years, I had a child's quintessential revelation: my mother had a whole life before I was even around.

Aunt Mae and Mom shared a close sisterhood, and my aunt had mother's infectious laugh and her low voice with the distinct Colorado accent. This precious time with Aunt Mae was the closest I would come to touching my mother's life as a vibrant young woman, crawling into the skin of her dreams. Sitting at the kitchen table, Mom's younger sister and I drank minted iced tea in the late summer afternoon. With that particular brilliant light from the Colorado Rockies pouring in

3

the windows, we laughed and cried looking at old photos and telling stories about my mother. I knew that Mom had studied art as a young woman, but Aunt Mae described whole new chapters of her sister's life.

"Of course you know that Jacquie was strikingly beautiful, and men were just crazy for her! She had more boyfriends than you could count, and she was always coming to me to help her sort out her love life." Aunt Mae laughed that husky laugh that could have been Mom's. "Gail darling, your mom always did her own thing. She skied on slopes that women never dared and she went to art school when most of her friends were going to secretarial school. And then, to top it off, Jacquie married a Protestant and went east. Believe me, your mom was a free spirit!" My aunt paused and gazed at me fondly, a smile playing at the corners of her mouth. "You certainly look like your mother, and you also seem to have inherited her independent spirit."

I grinned, happy to hear that my aunt thought I had something of my mother in me, and longed to drink up as many of Aunt Mae's recollections as she would serve. "Please tell me more. As much as you can."

"Though it might be hard for you to imagine, Gail dear, your mom was a very colorful bohemian living in the downtown lofts in Denver in the late 1930s. She painted in several mediums, she sculpted, and she was unusually successful for a young woman artist at that time.

"Your mother was very happy as an artist, Gail darling. She had all kinds of bohemian friends—painters, and poets, and writers. A lot like your life now, I would have to say." At twenty-four, I hadn't the slightest idea that Aunt Mae's accurate comparison of my mother's and my lifestyle was fraught with complex meaning that would take me the next three decades to fully understand.

My aunt rose and I could tell that she was really warming up to the story. "Wait a moment. I have some things I'd like to show you." While she went off to find more of her sister's story, my head was spinning with images of my mother in her loft in downtown Denver.

"Here's a recent newspaper article about Dori Carr Hutson, who was a friend of Jacquie's. They both painted in the 1930s, and they were well known for their fashion illustrations for the Denver Dry Goods. Back then, they could make good money doing this commercial art for the Denver newspapers, and then return to their studios to paint or sculpt." Aunt Mae handed me a long story from the Sunday magazine of the *Denver Times,* honoring the artist for her impressive sixty-five-year career. "One of her paintings is going into the Colorado National Museum of Women in the Arts. And look at this, Gail dear, here's a photo of Dori's first watercolor from 1928." As Aunt Mae guided me through the life story of this amazing woman, so like my mother at the start of her career, I was filled with that singular kind of sadness that is reserved for what could have been and never was. It was a sadness that stirred up things I didn't want to look at, including the fact that perhaps my mother had died long before her heart gave out, that there were many things I needed to know about Mom but never would.

"Something else I bet you never knew about your mom. Jacquie was the graphic artist for a well-known cartoon strip in the *Denver Post* called *Pigtail Pat and Her Pals.*" Aunt Mae took out some yellowed newspaper clippings.

As I took in the fading panels, I heard that distinctive husky laughter again. "Gosh, they still make me laugh. Look at these quirky smiles and poses, and the way the pigtails stick out at a crooked angle. I think your mom must have had a lot of fun doing these." I stared at my mother's rich animated images spilling off the page. So much life, so much vibrant imagination, so much talent. My eyes stung with tears.

Later, on the plane ride back to Boston, my mind drifted to a passage that haunts me by the poet Naomi Shihab Nye, writing about her mother. *Sometimes you were too sad to tell us why. Did other mothers cry? Sometimes the shadow of doubt rode your back and you could not shake it off. You can do it. The words went both ways. Were they ever enough? Who was the shadow? The self you might have been, without us?*

Home from my visit with Aunt Mae, I took out all the photos I owned of my mother as a young woman. In her bohemian days she was mysterious and beautiful, with bold hoop earrings, ruby red lipstick, and her curly hair swept up on top of her head. It's not just her physical beauty that startles; it's the fearless quality emanating from her pose and her eyes. Squinting at the image, I imagine an unbounded flame throwing off sparks of creativity and daring. There she is, Jacquie Walsh, before she was wife, mother, and full-time working mom. There she is, someone wild and exotic, unknown and fascinating to me. I pore over the pictures until they come alive and I find myself imagining her entire life as an artist in that Denver loft. She is bent over her table, her hands stained with paint, her face full of concentration, her mind on fire with colors and shapes, textures and juxtapositions. Completely at home with herself, the world disappears as she enters the space of her imagination, timeless and unbound. Later she will go out into the soft night, meeting with other artists and writers; they will drink coffee and engage in animated conversation.

When I think of my mother during that brief period of her life I want to freeze the film and leave her forever in her loft, with oil paints, watercolors, sundry brushes and canvases covering the wooden floor, and the smell of ink, paint, and creativity hanging heavy in the air. I want to surround her with friends who understand her essence and encourage her talents. I want to swap generations, giving Mom the freedom of choice that I had while I take the lack of options that informed her life. I desperately want to give my mother the life she never had, the life that she and most the women of her generation rarely allowed themselves to even dream of.

I have thought a great deal about my mother's dreams. When were they born and when did they die? What did her deepest longings feel like inside her heart, before that heart became burdened and broken? How many of Mom's dreams shattered because of her own doing, and which ones were stolen away by the dominant society? And then the question that surrounds all my other queries: can a daughter ever make up for her mother's loss?

Though I will never really know the answers to these things, what I do know for sure is that these questions live inside me, haunting me and deeply informing me. So much of my life has been shaped by what my mother betrayed, lost, or had stolen from her. I see now, from my vantage point of being almost sixty, that my life's work, my home and its surrounding landscape, my choice not to have children, and my close community in Woodstock, New York—one of the oldest artist colonies in America—have all been an attempt to return my mother's dreams to her. To prove that it's possible to live and grow old as an unbounded flame.

When Imagination Reigned

Brecks Lane and
the Bubble and Squeak

One of the greatest blessings in my life is that my mother's creative essence was fully intact during my childhood. Abundant with emotion and bold colors, unabashed spirituality and endless originality, Mom fully enjoyed being a woman. It wouldn't be until my early teenage years that she began to leave her authentic self behind and that I began trying to live for both of us. But in my early years her prolific imagination and artistry infused our home, making it a place of beauty and countless childhood adventures. Mom's love was so inseparable from her imagination that even now, when I think about her love for me, I am often transported to a particular memory where her abundant creativity filled me with happiness.

"Girls, how would you like to make puppets today?" she might ask, knowing full well how we adored these projects with her.

"Yes! Yes!" my sister Joanie and I would shout at the tops of our little lungs.

My mother spread all the materials for puppet making on our kitchen table and soon we had embarked an adventure that would unfold over many days.

"First we have to mix flour and water for the papier-mâché. It can't be too thick or too thin, but just right," she would say, teaching us the proper consistency for the gooey mix.

Next she showed us how to dip the cut strips of brown paper bag into the gooey mix, and then pull them along our skinny fingers until we had just the right amount to apply the strip onto the small balloon that would become the puppet's head. When the balloon was covered with plenty of strips, it was time to decide who the puppet would be.

"A magician," I might announce.

"I want a clown," Joanie might offer, before deciding the puppet was really a soulful dog.

Mom helped us shape the forehead, eyes, nose, mouth, and neck, her nimble fingers smoothing our clumsiness. When the head was finished, we let it dry. Coming back the next morning we pricked the balloon and found, to our utter amazement, that the gooey mix had hardened into a head. Now our mother got out her green painter's box and long wooden brushes.

"Let's paint the faces, and take your time, girls. Remember you can always paint over your mistakes," she said, anticipating the inevitable. Early on, Mom taught us that mistakes and creativity were close sisters who loved each other's company. She helped us paint the puppet's face with long black eye lashes, full red lips, and pink dimples. She knew just when to let us paint on our own and when to intervene in order to avoid catastrophe. Soon out would come her wooden sewing box, a treasure chest full of scraps of green velvet, red corduroy, flannel plaids from my father's old work shirts, brass buttons, and small bits of lace. After we chose our own bits of fabric, she helped us cut the pattern and then sewed the tiny costume on her black and gold Singer sewing machine.

"Now, girls, be very careful, these are very sharp," Mom would say, placing the big darning needles in our small hands. Sewing the costume onto the puppet heads was always a little tricky. After we did the best we could, our mother covered our clumsy stitches with high lace collars or miniature scarves tied stylishly around the puppet's neck.

My favorite part was when we glued on the puppet's hair, using brightly colored yarn, or, best of all, small blond curls of wood from my father's shop. The final results were both inspired and primitive. Clowns with clashing plaid suits and electric blue hair, magicians with gold buttons completely covering their velvet costumes, and dogs with ears down to their feet. Under Mom's constant encouragement, this kind of project might go on for weeks, and include making a stage, and then creating and performing our own highly original puppet shows. During these adventures my mother was a natural teacher of creative collaboration, modeling the high art of give and take, the careful balance of individuality and teamwork.

Similar days and weeks were spent with our mother teaching us the fine art of piñata making, creating our own series of paper dolls, and constructing books of pressed leaves and flowers. When we needed a break from scissors and glue, we might bake blueberry pies and end up with tongues turned the color of indigo. No matter what we had created, my mother's response was always the same. "How wonderful!" she would say. And each time her enthusiasm filled my tiny heart with the bright belief that I, and whatever creation came forth from me, were indeed wonderful. My mother's imagination was utterly contagious, pouring out of her with such ease and generosity that I was forever imbued with this richness. Of course, I thought all mothers showed their daughters the doorway into their imagination, ushered them into a world that was totally their own and that no one could ever take away. How little I knew how precious this was. How little I knew how soon my mother's rich creativity would recede into the background, replaced by the darker forces that shaped so many women's lives at that time. Complicated currents were at play, currents involving money and striving and fitting in, tensions in her marriage, struggles with her devout Catholicism, not to mention a conservative society just waiting to steal away her untamed imagination.

But there were many good years before those forces entered Mom's life. A brown-haired Irish beauty with hazel eyes and a contagious laugh, as a young artist my mother dressed with great flair, mixing bright floral skirts with white peasant blouses, then donning canvas shoes with long black laces that crisscrossed up her slender legs. It's easy to see how my father fell head over heels in love with Jacqueline Walsh and brought her back east from Denver. Mom was the only member of her rowdy tribe of eight siblings to leave Colorado for the East Coast, not to mention the only member of the close-knit Irish Catholic Walsh family to marry a Protestant. There she was in the early 1940s, a radiant young woman suddenly uprooted from her family, her faith, and her place. Could my mother possibly have known all she was leaving behind or what she had put into motion by making such radical choices? Did she have the slightest idea that her blatant independence placed her a full generation ahead of herself? Did she have any awareness of the potent societal forces just waiting to put an end to her boldness? Ironically, long after her death I would be awed and inspired by these early choices, interpreting them as a carte blanche for my own independence and a blueprint for my fierce commitment to choice.

Although much was unknown, one thing was certain for my mother. She was crazy in love with my father. In their marriage portrait my parents are a dashing couple, Father lean and handsome in his army captain's uniform and Mother luminous in her white velvet and satin wedding gown. Their honeymoon photos show them arm in arm in the Colorado Rockies with stylish 1940s fur ski parkas cocooning their heads, skis resting against their shoulders, fresh and eager to fulfill their dreams. Shortly after they were married Mom and Pop moved to Pennsylvania to be closer to Dad's mother. Soon after they settled in Pennsylvania and then Delaware, my brother Jimmy was born. I came five years later, in 1949, and my sister Joanie just fourteen months after me. Then the Straub family moved to Brecks Lane, a close-knit neighborhood near the banks of the historic Brandywine River just outside Wilmington, Delaware.

The rest of my mother's years would be shaped by our life on Brecks Lane. The rugged Rocky Mountains of her Colorado youth were replaced by the green of the Brandywine River Valley. Mom never lost her wonder at this lushness, especially in the spring when the whole valley turned various shades of chartreuse, blossoming with pinks and purples. "Can you believe how green it is, darling?" she would say to me. "Just look at this! It's intoxicating isn't it?" Although she was deeply nourished by the lush green she had never known in her childhood, my mother also profoundly missed all she had lost when she left Colorado. I would not fully understand the extent of her losses until much later, when they affected me so deeply that I would spend the rest of my life trying to make up for them.

My Brecks Lane childhood was as abundant with happiness as the green in the Brandywine River Valley. Brecks Lane was a real 1950s community before close, engaged neighborhoods became an endangered species. We shared cookouts and baseball games, pumpkin carving and Christmas caroling, vintage circuses and talent shows with entire families joining in, lots of family parties, and a genuine caring for each other.

In the early years our Brecks Lane house was full of joy and vibrant with life. My sister Joanie and I were best friends, and tomboy rascals. A star athlete and student, my older brother Jimmy was our idol. My father was a tall handsome teacher loved by students and faculty alike at the prestigious private school where he taught.

Brecks Lane was on a steep hill making its way down to the Brandywine River, where the old powder mills that supplied gunpowder for the Civil War still existed. Our house at 198½ Brecks Lane was a white wood frame with a beautiful bluestone chimney running up the center of the house. Mom liked to say that the house seemed to fit our family like a glove. There was a comfortable den where we could all lazily sit and watch television, a living room that showcased the antiques that my father was famous for restoring, our kitchen with its "utility island" of sinks, stove, and dishwasher that was 1950s state of the art, a long narrow dining room framed with tall windows looking out onto the screen porch and Mom's garden, and three bedrooms and two baths upstairs. When we were children my father would say to Joanie and me, "You want to know something wonderful about our house? This living room we're sitting in at this very moment used to be a tiny toll station at the top of Brecks Lane. And you know what?" He would ask us, his eyes growing big, "The toll keeper was a troll." I sincerely hoped this troll still lived somewhere in our rambling old attic, and I felt sure the half in the 198½ belonged to him.

Our home was a true creative partnership between my parents. Every room was graced with my father's hand-crafted furniture. There were walnut lamps, a long maple Shaker dining room table, four-poster cherrywood beds, and the unique two-seated desk that Pop had made for the inseparable Joanie and me. My mother's watercolors, bright ceramic-tiled tables, and vibrant sense of color seemed the perfect complement.

Just as with Mom's artistry, I naïvely assumed that all homes were this vibrant, and that all parents shared this love of beauty. Many years later my husband David and I filled our house with handmade wood and local art. We both believed that attention to beauty was one way to stay sane. My parents had taught me well.

Along with this care for loveliness, Mom really knew how to make a house a warm haven of belonging. Rocky, our honey-colored cocker spaniel with his tiny tail in perpetual contented motion, was the king of our house. Fully aware that my mother adored him, Rocky got away with murder, sleeping on good living room couches, messing up freshly polished floors, and dragging an abundance of poor creatures into the house for Mom's approval. There were big cookie jars full of treats and pitchers of raspberry Kool-Aid, a noisy washing machine and Benny Goodman's big band playing on the RCA record player. Our Brecks Lane house had ample flowering bushes, and Mom placed pitchers of fresh flowers on Pop's shining handmade tables. And there was plenty of space for us to spread out and make a mess. Our home always seemed to hum with a rhythm that was both orderly and improvisational, inviting creativity. As soon as Mom died this ineffable sense of belonging vanished. It would be many years before I fully understood the power of my mother's presence, the invisible glue that held everything together. Her presence was the feminine force that created a shelter from the storms of life, a safe haven where I could grow and dream and become myself.

We got to live in our house only because Pop taught at the prestigious Tower Hill School and Brecks Lane was where some of the teachers lived. My parents paid one hundred dollars a month in rent, and it was a lot of money for them. Spanning kindergarten through twelfth grade, Tower Hill School educated the sons and daughters of the elite wealthy families—the Du Ponts, the Cravens, and the Carpenters, along with a few others—who owned Wilmington, Delaware. Whether living on Brecks Lane meant that we were extremely blessed or constantly reminded of how much we didn't have depended on my mother's mood. On some days Mom knew that by almost any standards our home was comfortable and lovely, more than most teachers' families ever dreamed of. But on other days, the insidious comparison with the Du Pont mansions left my mother blind to everything she had. As if to underscore the terrible ambiguity that ate away at my mother, our house was situated exactly across the street from the long winding driveway leading to one of the Du Pont family estates. At that spot in the road, from one driveway across to the other, stretched the tension between great wealth and simple comfort that would deeply inform my childhood experience and later my entire worldview.

Mom must have understood Freud's famous words, "Who has been secure in his mother's love, will be secure through life," because she managed to get the delicate balance of nurturing guidance and freedom just about right. Deeply intuitive, her mothering didn't seem to subscribe to any specific guidelines; rather she followed her instincts as she doled out the dosages of discipline or leniency. Under her careful direction she had awakened my imagination and she knew it needed plenty of space to flourish. When she had things to do she sent Joanie and me out to play, and our tomboy wings took flight in the trees, brooks, and fields around Brecks Lane. By the time I was four, the landscape had already claimed my heart, had already become a central comfort and healer. Here in the lushness of the Brandywine River Valley, my lifelong love affair with the natural world was born.

Younger by only fourteen months, my sister Joanie was my constant comrade in childhood's innocent abandon. We were often mistaken as twins and indeed we were inseparable.

Dressed in scruffy blue jeans and red striped tee shirts with our identical Dutch boy haircuts, we were two rascals looking for trouble.

Shinnying our skinny legs way up over trunks and out onto long branches, we explored every tree in our childhood landscape. We especially loved the sprawling old beech tree at the end of our yard, whose branches reached out over the small brook called the Pancake Run. After hanging upside down like monkeys in the old tree we followed the Pancake Run down to the Brandywine River with its old stone mills. Along the Pancake Run we collected stores of treasure: pebbles, flowers, moss, bark, and insects. Arriving at the Brandywine soaked and filthy, we felt no less important than Lewis and Clark.

Dangling our bare feet in the river one day, watching the giant turning wheel of the Civil War powder mill, I ask Joanie, "What do you think it was like living back then?"

"I bet it was much more interesting."

"Why would it be more interesting than now?"

"Because they had to figure more things out back then. Everything seems too easy now, as if it's all been worked out."

"I am glad it's easier. I don't really like things hard," I said unabashedly. "I just want to have adventures."

Two tomboys sitting on the edge of the Brandywine and already our lives were turning inexorably toward our futures, turning like the big old wheel of the powder mill. Joanie would become the scientist, a wetlands ecologist whose joy is to figure things out. And I would become the entrepreneur having adventures around the world. Mom's instinctual balance of nurturance and independence had planted a marvelous combination of confidence and curiosity in Joanie and me. Clearly she knew that our imagination flourished both under her guidance as well as in the untamed freedom of the natural world.

Parallel to the Pancake Run, across a large field in the back of our house, was what my mother called the Bubble and

Squeak Railroad. She refused to tell us the real name of the railroad line, and I am glad she never did. Even today I don't now if it has a real name. Mom knew if we weren't in the Pancake Run we'd be out back on the Bubble and Squeak.

Joanie and I took handfuls of Oreos from the smiling piggy cookie jar and made thick peanut butter and marshmallow fluff sandwiches. We packed our picnics into our red bandanas and tied them onto our hobo sticks. Off down the Bubble and Squeak we went, hobo sticks over our shoulders, our small hearts thumping with excitement.

I remember arriving near the large railroad bridge and pronouncing, "Joanie, look at all these old green wine bottles and piles of crushed cigarette butts. It's a sure sign there are real hobos nearby. I dare you to peak underneath the bridge and look smack into the eyes of a hobo."

"You're just afraid, I bet," she said.

"No, I'm not."

"Well, let's go together then."

Inevitably one of us would peek under the bridge, and then we'd both scream, taking off like bats out of hell, running all the way home. No matter how many times we repeated this adventure, we never discussed if we had actually seen a real hobo. Even today, as women in our late fifties, Joanie and I can easily reengage in this willing suspension of disbelief, immersing ourselves once again in the infinite possibilities of childhood innocence, in that luscious field of fertile imagination where our mother taught us how to feel at home.

The frontiers of our adventures expanded with our years. Just beyond the Pancake Run and the Bubble and Squeak lay what we had named the Big Field. This was our big brother Jimmy's territory, and we knew it. With his gang of Brecks Lane cronies Jimmy played endless games of touch football, baseball, and whiffle ball. Our brother was a champion athlete and both the younger and older boys looked up to him, as did Joanie and I. When we were finally allowed to play in the Big Field, Jimmy lovingly looked after us, as he had for much of our childhood.

On warm evenings, passionate games of capture the flag took place in the Big Field. Older boys from outside the safe womb of my Brecks Lane neighborhood joined in for these heated contests. They might as well have been Hell's Angels just in from Philadelphia as far as I was concerned. I stayed close to my tall brother, who chatted easily with them, until the excitement of the game inevitably swept me up. I was in heaven, running fast—faster, faster—across the long field, so free and untamed. It is this image of myself, as a spirited tomboy flying across the Big Field, that offers an eloquent symbol of the days at Brecks Lane when imagination reigned, and both my mother and I were free to be the fullest expressions of our unbridled selves.

St. Joseph's and the Wilmington Dry Goods

When I have warm easy memories of Mom I almost always see her happily puttering around the Brecks Lane house engaging us in a myriad of creative projects. But when I have more complicated thoughts about my mother I picture her kneeling at mass at St. Joseph's Church. A devout Catholic, my mother is achingly beautiful, wistful and far away, sitting in the yellow stucco Catholic church where she attended mass every Sunday, prayed the stations of the cross most Fridays, and rarely missed confession on Saturday. Formed by her strong Irish Catholic roots, her devotion was most likely equally inspired by her enormous need for the inner quiet time her faith afforded her. Indeed, the only time I can picture my mother still and unto herself was when she was in church. As the outer demands of her life became more complex it's a wonder she didn't move into St. Joseph's.

Sunday was a big deal in our house, and as a family we attended mass every week without fail. For Christmas, Easter, and other important holy days, mass started long before Sunday itself. Right up until our high school years my mother would drag Joanie and me to the Wilmington Dry Goods to buy our hats, dresses, and shoes for high mass at St. Joseph's. To this day, the man St. Joseph and the Wilmington Dry Goods are forever entwined in my mind.

"Now girls, remember we're shopping downtown and you have to stay very close to me at all times," she would say sternly.

We were already painfully aware that the Wilmington Dry Goods was in the wrong part of town and our rich classmates, who were definitely Protestant, not Catholic, were shopping way uptown at Lilly Pulitzer and The Villager.

I hated shopping but I was keenly fascinated by the Wilmington Dry Goods. The floors of the store were rough wood and the whole place smelled musty, as if I'd just opened up a giant old trunk. And then there were the rows and rows and rows of dresses, shoes, hats, and purses. While Mom tried on her outfits, I perched like a little mouse under the racks of clothes and watched the other shoppers. People had black skin, women dressed differently from my mother, and the children my age didn't look like my friends at Tower Hill. Their faces told stories that opened doors to new worlds. It was as if I had entered my first foreign culture, and I yearned to know more.

When it was time to shop for Joanie and me, our mother started with shoes. "Child, where did you get feet like these? They don't even touch the ground," she would say after unsuccessfully trying to fit the fourth pair of shoes onto my absurdly high-arched narrow feet.

"They're just like Pop's feet," I said, having examined my father's long, strange feet many times. Years later my first boyfriend would tell me I had feet like Jesus.

After shoes we would do dresses, and by the time we got to hats Joanie and I were fed up and cranky beyond repair.

"None of my friends have to wear hats to church. They don't even go to church for that matter. I hate being Catholic," I shouted down the long rows of the Wilmington Dry Goods.

"Hush, child!" hissed my mother.

But I was just getting started. "Why can't I be like the other girls at Tower Hill? Why do I always have to go to church and why can't I buy my clothes at The Villager uptown?"

As my frustration rose above the pastel pink straw hats, I hadn't a clue that my mother felt more like an outsider than I did. That she, far more than I, wished she could wear the expensive clothes that the wealthy Wilmington mothers sported at every occasion. Nor did I have the slightest notion that the sharp tension between her faith and the unfairness of life was just beginning to wedge itself into my mother's heart. For now these currents ran gently inside her, but before too long they would create a raging river that tore asunder her sense of self as well as her marriage. For now my mother simply replied with strong emotion, "You know perfectly well that we can't afford those kinds of clothes and you also know that every person needs a spiritual foundation and that's why you go to mass. Here, try on this hat with the white ribbon," she steamed, shoving the hat onto my hot little head. "Now, I don't want to hear one more word out of you!"

So it went until Sunday morning, when Mother lined us up like chickens in our best hats and gloves, suits, and ties. Since it was never an option to miss Sunday mass, Mom had Pop convert to Catholicism, undoubtedly as part of the deal they struck when they married. Of course Mom would never have to know that once she died my father never again set foot inside a Catholic church, or any church for that matter. For now, off we would go in our family's old woody station wagon up over the hill to St. Joseph's Church. Mom was elegant in her navy blue high-waisted suit topped off with a navy straw bonnet and scented with her Sunday perfume. Nine o'clock mass was followed by catechism class with the impressive sisters of St. Joseph's, then home to a special Sunday brunch of eggs and decadent sticky buns, which we all ate with great relish.

Over the years I tried my best to be a good Catholic, mostly because I knew it was so important to my mother. On Saturday afternoons when I entered the dark confessional, with its stuffy smell and strange screen separating me from the priest, I always felt like another person from another time long ago. I imagined myself as an old woman, likely from Dublin, hunched over in a black shawl, widowed and miserable, coming to the priest for help. But then came the problem of confessing the sins of this poor Irish widow, and there I was at a loss. Alas, I always had to come back to my own life and my own sins.

"Bless me, Father, for I have sinned. It has been one week since my last confession." The familiar words recited at the beginning of the ritual came out easily, but then I had to pull myself back from Dublin into the smelly cramped cubicle and try to remember the bad things I had done.

"These are my sins. I disobeyed my mother once, I yelled at my sister Joanie six times, I had many dirty thoughts, and I said 'damn' four times." It was usually some variation on this short list of wrongdoings that innocently gushed out, and I remember thinking even then that the process of confession was very strange. What I really wanted to say to the priest hidden behind the Plexiglas screen full of holes was, "Why am I, a carefree young girl, telling you, a man in a black suit with a white collar, all these private things that seem like normal parts of life?" But I never had the courage to ask the priest such a thing.

I attended mass with my mother every Sunday from the age of five until the day I left home for college. After I went away to college I would only rarely return to mass, wandering into an especially beautiful church in some corner of the globe where I was traveling or working. My spiritual inclinations unfolded like a baby boomer Rorschach: hippie, feminist, social activist, Buddhist, and finally Buddhist Christian. My iconoclasm notwithstanding, I see that all those years of Sunday masses wove an invisible space between my mother and me that would far outlast her physical existence, an eternal space where contradictions were welcome, where joy and sorrow lived as close sisters.

It was in this space, many years later, that I would be able to fit together the warm and intimate aspects of my mother with the sad and distant parts. I can imagine us now, just the two of us sitting close to each other in the well-worn pews at St. Joseph's. With the unmistakable scent of incense and votive candles wafting around us, surrounded by the stations of the cross depicting Christ's death and resurrection in graphic detail, I hear Mom saying, "Darling, faith and devotion are important but you must understand they cannot guarantee a smooth or happy life. It's only when we can let go of our most precious desires and hardened righteousness that mature faith is born. And this kind of devotion is usually hard won." Though it took me a full three decades after she died, I now see how my mother's innocent devotion matured into a profound faith over the years. That the church had committed a profound injustice against her following Joanie's birth, I would not learn until long after her death. Fired in the kiln of suffering as a result of this injustice, my mother's faith gave her a mystic's heart capable of holding such vast contradictions as abiding belief in the midst of betrayal, generous love for those very ones who have taken something precious away from you, and joie de vivre in the stark presence of death.

This mystic's heart was soon to be broken, the pieces shattering around me in such profound disarray that I would run far, far away for a long, long time. But, in the end, because my mother had left me the footprints of her mysticism, I could retrace her steps back to the wisdom that she had left me: that each life requires a baptism of impossible contradictions and that mature faith requires us to bow deeply at the feet of paradox. I have come to believe that during all those hours that Mom spent in confession, at mass, and praying stations of the cross, she was in communion with the sacred feminine. The holy lady was assuring her that by holding life and death, pleasure and pain, and hope and despair with equal tenderness and respect, we can find peace and freedom.

I'll never know how disappointed she might have been that I didn't become a good Catholic, but I know that my own passionate love affair with the inexplicable runs through the same veins as my mother's devotion. I know that my faith in the reconciliation of opposites would become the very heart of my work as a teacher, the very essence of what fed my students' great spiritual hunger. Born in the lap of my mother, my faith has flown far from the pews of St. Joseph's and returned me to the arms of the Great Mother.

Pop and the
Tower Hill School

Starting with first grade, my childhood day began by walking with my father from our house on Brecks Lane over to the Tower Hill School. A year later Joanie joined us, and with me on one side of Pop, she on the other, we crossed the Pancake Run and the Bubble and Squeak and walked through the Big Field. Then we came to the small road graced by the various estates, stunning stone mansions, tall hedges, and manicured gardens of the Du Ponts and the Cravens and leading directly to Tower Hill, the school created to educate these families. In seventh grade by then, Jimmy was deemed old enough to make the fifteen-minute walk by himself. Only truly inclement weather stopped us, otherwise one very tall Straub could be seen with two small Straubs moving through the seasons of golden yellow leaves, frost etched on long gray branches, and finally the gown of chartreuse in all its glory. I adored these walks with Pop, which lasted right up until high school, when, busy fussing with my hair and clothes, I was always too late to join him. My lifelong passion for walking was born on these early jaunts where nature, silence, and wonderful talks with loved ones moved together in such lovely harmony.

Arriving before school began, Joanie and I had a few more precious minutes with our father. He was the shop teacher at Tower Hill, and his spacious workroom enchanted me. There, he donned his khaki smock and turned the splendid walnut, pine, maple, and cherry wood into lamps, tables, four-poster beds, and sailboats. Amidst the pungent smells of sawdust, paint, and shellac my tall, handsome father became a magician, his long slender hands silently offering the world evidence of beauty. How could such tender beauty have come from a man who at the age of twelve, during the height of the Great Depression, had watched his own father shoot himself in the head as he and his mother stood helplessly by? It is a question I have never been able to answer. My Grammie Straub was left a single mother, alone and destitute. Soon after, my father's younger sister died of tuberculosis. My father never spoke of these things but his stoicism gave him a gravitas that drew people toward him as if he understood some deep secret about life.

Equally loved by students and faculty, my father was born to be a teacher. He was as comfortable helping first graders make comical spotted giraffes, pink pigs, and brown camels as he was mentoring his older students as they learned to build handsome furniture and repair almost anything. During special evening classes, Pop helped his fellow faculty repair and refinish old tables, chairs, and desks until they looked better than new. A passionate and caring instructor, my father imprinted in me a love of teaching that would shape my future calling.

Sometimes the parents of his students brought the precious antiques that filled their wealthy homes into my father's shop.

"Jim, this is a vintage chestnut trestle table but you'd never know it with these terrible layers of paint."

"Let me see what I can do," he would say, smoothing his hands over the surface of the table.

"Jim, this spinning wheel is the genuine article, well over a hundred years old, but the spindle is missing. Would there be any way you could make a spindle?"

"Well, I've never been asked to make a spindle before," he would laugh, "but I can give it a try."

Later they would come back for their antiques and express amazement at the transformation my father had brought about. With its sawdust-covered floors, high-pitched singing of the band saw, and the fragrant smell of fresh-cut pine and walnut, Jim Straub's shop was a place where things were built, repaired, and refinished. It was a place where even the most broken things, like my father's own life, could become whole again.

Pop's good fortune at landing a teaching job at the Tower Hill School can't be overestimated. A small private country day school, Tower Hill was and is a force to be reckoned with, an oasis of excellence in the wasteland of American education. My brother Jimmy followed in my father's footsteps as a teacher and a coach at Tower Hill, and I can still feel the indelible mark of excellence my teachers left on me during the fifties and sixties. Along with my parents, my thirteen years at Tower Hill were the primary forces that shaped my values and the path I would follow in life.

Winking at me from behind a desk, in front of a blackboard, or on the athletic field, I hear the cadence of their voices—Miss West, Madame Cleve, Mr. Borgeault, Mr. Wood, and Coach Hughes—scolding, cajoling, and inspiring me. While some took a gentle approach—"Gail, have you have you finished Rachel Carson's *Silent Spring*? Emerson and Emily Dickinson are waiting for you"—and some were not quite as delicate—"Wake up, Straub, you meatball. Now that you've finished reading *Ulysses*, describe the tension between hope and despair in Joyce's masterpiece"—all expected no less than my best. Each of them mentored me in a different way and each of them remained immanently present in the life choices I would make.

How marvelous to leave the intensity of Joyce and go down the hallway to Mr. Borgeault's music room, where the popular and eccentric teacher in a polka-dot bow tie always found his classroom crammed with enthusiastic students. Mr. B's unabashed passion for Bach and Stravinsky, as well as the Beatles and the Stones, deserves the most credit for my lifelong love affair with music. And then, to finish the day speaking French with Madame Cleve was just about heaven for me. Mesmerized by the sonorous beauty of her language, I loved everything foreign about Madame herself. She dressed in the old European style, with silver jewelry on her fitted black wool dresses, offering a dramatic contrast next to her snow-white hair. Her fine leather heels buttoned up to her ankles and she smelled of fresh lavender, all the while teaching me to love Camus and Proust and Paris. If Madame Cleve hadn't fled Europe and the Nazis and ended up as my French teacher, it's likely that I might never have led my life as a global citizen with a voracious cultural appetite.

My joy at Tower Hill's emphasis on both intellectual and physical excellence foreshadowed my own prominent involvement in the holistic movement that would become popular in years to come. As a young woman I played team sports from sixth grade on, learning the values of teamwork and the intrinsic relationship between physical and mental discipline. Though I had no idea how visionary this was at the time, the girls' teams were given just as much attention as the boys'. Here were some of the earliest seeds in my lifelong commitment to feminism. With sports, Joanie and I found a perfect way to channel our tomboy energy. Each in our turn, we became captain of our lacrosse team, leading it to a string of undefeated seasons. Our coach was the fierce and charismatic Ed Hughes, who treated us no differently than if he had been working with young men. Strategic and grueling, our daily two-hour practices found Coach Hughes teaching us complex patterns of footwork, passes, and fakes. We left our rival teams baffled and beaten by our intricate plays, which we fondly entitled Mick Jagger, Ringo, and Mr. Tambourine Man. Coach's voice is as unforgettable today as it was on my high school playing field. "You called this play, Miss Straub, and you're one of the fastest girls in the school. How could you possibly, possibly, have missed the goal? Get your act together! And if you don't watch your footwork you'll end up with another nasty black eye, like the one you got in the last game."

I still marvel at how blessed I was for all my years at Tower Hill. The gifts bestowed—my own high standards of excellence and discipline partnered with a boundless curiosity and a desire to give back—are an embarrassment of riches. They say a parent wants nothing more than to offer their children what they never had. The contrast between Pop's childhood of poverty and loss, and his children's extraordinary education at the school where he gave so much of his life is a gap so wide and deep it leaves me staring breathless into its mystery.

Mom Leaves
Her Own House

Over those years at Tower Hill my father managed to stay true to himself, making his peace with Wilmington society without feeling he needed to measure up or fit in. But as the years passed, my mother longed to be part of the high-society parties and conversations. The more she tried to belong, the more she began to leave behind her true self, a free spirit with a wide imagination and a decided joie de vivre, in order to try to fit into Wilmington's stuffy society. When I look at pictures of my mother during my own teenage years, she looks stiff and tired. Her vibrant sense of color and style is no longer evident, her stylish creations having been replaced with conservative suits. Her body language is no longer relaxed and graceful, but now appears rigid with tension. Her feminine has been replaced by the masculine, her natural sense of herself as a woman has disappeared into an imitation of a man. When did her need to belong to a conservative male-driven society begin to steal away her innate female wisdom? When, exactly, does the gradual death of the feminine begin for any of us?

I see now that there were two nearly equal halves to my life with my mother. First were my childhood years, when Mom was at home with herself and her bountiful imagination flooded my Brecks Lane days like sunlight. Then, somewhere around my thirteenth year, Mom began to leave her own house. Until she died ten years later, my mother left behind more and more of her authentic self—the paints spread out on the kitchen table, her comfort with her vibrant originality and independent spirit, the ease with which she stood up to my father, the love of her home and the feeling that her life was rich enough. Slowly but surely the subtle interior compass that guided her was replaced by exterior standards and outer status symbols. Is it possible that my entire search has been to reconcile the stark contrast between these two halves of my life with my mother? To understand how our interior truth is abducted by society's mass norms, to understand how we lose ourselves.

Now the light-filled rooms of my childhood along with the rooms of my mother's soul began to fall into dark shadows. Why did she so thoroughly abandon her bohemian loft, suffused with rich creativity and surrounded by a community of friends who encouraged her free spirit and her art? What led her to close the door on her penetrating intuition, which had guided both her mothering and her own strong independence? How did her faith change from openhearted mysticism into prayers of exhaustion? When did the highly imaginative sense of collaboration that had been at the center of our childhood adventures turn into never-ending lists of things to do? At what point then did she turn her back on her interior life? Was Mom simply doing the best she could? How much of my mother's abandonment was her own doing, and how much was she at the mercy of a culture that routinely betrays the feminine? The answers to these questions are of course so complex and intertwined that it's impossible to know exactly where my mother's unraveling began.

The fact is, I don't know and I never will know.

What is clear is that my mother's spirit began to die as she lost her connection to her innate female wisdom. As she betrayed her heart's instincts and her creative priorities, as her need to fit in replaced her originality, and as she turned away from the interior life and more and more toward exterior status, each of these was a small death. Soon her body, too, would begin to die. My mother's story is so many of our stories, both men and women. I want to believe that there is a way that I can make up for all that she, and you, and I have lost. It is this fragile yet fierce belief that inspires so much of my own search.

After Mom died, in a moment of rare emotional intimacy, my father said to me, "Our marriage began to suffer when Wilmington society started to tempt your mother into wanting something better than the life we had. She had been happy up till then." So unusual was this moment of personal revelation, and so resonant was this truth, that I recorded his words verbatim in my tattered journal from the period of my early twenties. Was it cultural pressure that squeezed the free spirit out of my mother and replaced it with the pursuit of Wilmington's conservative high-society values? Did Mom's need to belong compel her to choose outer status and conformity over her inner creative impulses? I wonder if the radical nature of her three-part uprooting—from faith, family, and place—increased her need to belong, to put down roots. Perhaps this loneliness left her particularly vulnerable to being swept up by the most formidable group around her, even though it held none of her core values. Like my mother, how many women have given up their essence in order to belong, only later to discover that there is no possibility of belonging when there is no authentic self?

Our dinner table was the site of countless loud arguments reflecting the growing tension between my parents. An image that will last forever is one of Mom rushing home from work to prepare her famous chili that we all loved. She is heaping the servings into the blue-and-white Chinese weeping willow bowls, for her family who eats like a team of horses. Seated around the cherrywood table that Pop had made, the five of us are catching up on the day's news. "Oh, Jim, I got the prettiest cocktail dress today. It's black velvet with an elegant satin trim. It was marked down to half price at thirty-five dollars. Wait till you see it, girls! I'm going to wear it this Friday to the Winterthur Museum fundraiser." Mom's eyes are sparkling with pleasure, her excitement hard to resist.

Pop does resist it, though. "We can't possibly afford thirty-five dollars for a dress, Jacquie." He speaks calmly and arrogantly, continuing to eat his chili.

Mom immediately stops eating, already beside herself. "Well, I need this dress for the cocktail party Friday night. What am I supposed to wear?"

"For chrissake Jacquie, I don't even want to go to the stupid cocktail party. Who needs it? I'm always bored at these things anyway." My father's voice is brimming with superiority.

"Well, I sure want to go! I enjoy these parties a lot, even if you don't. Why do you have to be so goddamn antisocial?"

"Oh, get off my back. Just go to the damn party!" And Pop storms off, leaving Jimmy, Joanie, and me to sit silently with our crying mother.

Money was the most common theme of their arguments and a constant strain in our house. Both my parents worked full-time, and my father had an extra weekend job as a guide at the Hagley Museum. By the time we were fourteen, Jimmy, Joanie, and I had part-time jobs in order to help out with our expenses. No matter how hard all five Straubs worked, the demon of not enough money rarely left us alone. It's a very fine line as to how much of this tension was due to true financial pressure and how much came from the insidious comparison with how the Du Ponts lived.

Far worse, however, than the money disagreements were the fights when my brother and sister and I took sides with my father, ganging up on my mother. I am loath to admit the powerful seduction of my father's rational condescension toward my mother's emotional outbursts. Like most families in the fifties and sixties, dare I say even today, Mom carried the emotional life for all of us. Pop was stoic and intellectual, while Mom was high-strung with feelings of every shade and texture. Whether the discussion involved sports, politics, Tower Hill gossip, or even Wilmington society, my father always knew best. We were swept along in the tide of his linear arguments rushing over my mother's sensitive feelings. Over and over I can hear the phrase intoned in my father's most condescending voice, "Jacquie, you don't know anything about this, so just stay out of it."

"Yeah, Mom, you don't understand why the Phillies are on a winning streak. You don't even know the rules of baseball. Do you even know who Sandy Kofax is?" Jimmy or Joanie or I might add with cruel arrogance.

"No, I don't. But I know you all enjoy watching the Phillies. And I love watching the Tower Hill baseball games because your brother is the captain and star catcher. That's enough for me," she would say, her cheeks flushed pink from our attack.

"That's not the point, Mom. We're discussing the genius of Sandy Kofax and how he's changing baseball history. Geez, will you never get with it?" I am a pitch-perfect imitation of my father's disgust.

During these onslaughts, Mom would often get up from

the dinner table before finishing her food, and start doing the dishes as the four of us continued to eat the meal she had rushed home to prepare after a long day at work. As she abandoned more of her intrinsic emotional intelligence, my mother stopped standing up for herself in these arguments. Yes, yet another death of the soul. The rational masculine ganged up on the solitary emotional feminine seems a perfect symbol for that time in the late 1950s. Yet Mom's inability to stand up for herself because she was alone and without support is still poignantly true for many, many women. As I would eventually learn, reclaiming the conscious feminine is partly a solitary journey, but some phases can only be traveled with the support of community. I would find that support among a strong network of feminist friends, and this was one of the most significant differences between my mother's generation and mine. It is a difference I pray the next generation of women will not take for granted.

Underneath all of my parents' arguments was the tension of my mother wanting more and Pop feeling he couldn't give it to her. The more trapped my father felt, the more he had to be right. The more he felt he couldn't give her what she so deeply desired, the more the rational masculine had to trump the emotional feminine. And the faster my mother vacated her rooms of interior feelings and immeasurable caring, the faster I moved permanently into the rooms of my father's house, exterior intellect and measurable accomplishment. How little I knew what a long road it would be before I reinhabited the chambers of my heart. I knew nothing about the fact that I would never be happy until I lived harmoniously in both the rooms of my head and my heart, passing between them as easily as two equally cherished spaces. I had no idea that I could not become a woman until I stood up for my mother at the table of life.

Surely part of Mom's yearning for "a better life" was the sharp contrast between how she spent her days and the way many of the wealthy Tower Hill mothers spent theirs. Many of these mothers didn't want or need to work. Even without jobs they often still had professional help with their kids, their house, and their cooking. This left time for golf at the Wilmington Country Club, antique hunting in the Brandywine River Valley, visiting the splendid Longwood Gardens, and other hobbies of the privileged. Meanwhile, Mom had jumped two decades into the era of superwoman, raising three children, running a household, and working full-time. I can still see my mother waxing our kitchen floor every weekend with the old General Electric waxer with the big brusher wheels. Mom is polishing the black and white linoleum floor with fury and intensity, and I hear her thoughts as if she is shouting them above the terrible moaning of the heavy machine. "I will *never* have enough hours in the day. I will *never* have time for myself." And she never did.

Countless weekday evenings I would hear my mother charge into the house from her job at Stockwell's Antiques. Camel's hair coat still on her back and purse still over her arm, she threw a pan onto the stove, frantically thawing the frozen pork chops in the hot frying pan, before Pop and the three of us would barge into the kitchen ravenous and ready for dinner. After dinner, while Jimmy, Joanie, and I took cleanup detail, Mom was often so exhausted that she would fall asleep on Pop's lap as he read the paper. A hopelessly self-centered adolescent, I stood by as the demon of exhaustion strangled my mother's vibrant imagination and creativity.

Being a typical household in the early sixties we didn't discuss our feelings, as would later become the mode in the seventies and eighties, giddy with therapy fever. But whether discussed or not, feelings are still felt. Far too young to have the conceptual understanding of what was happening to my mother, my heart and body fully registered the turmoil. During my early teenage years I had increasing difficulty seeing the blackboard. Sent to the nurse's office for an eye exam, I could only make out the largest line right below the big E on the eye chart. The nurse called my condition a sudden and radical loss of sight. Is it too glib to say I no longer wanted to see what was going on around me? In the same period I went from being a high honors student to just maintaining a B average.

By the time I was in high school my mother's emotional abandonment became vastly more complicated by her physical condition. Now her fatigue was not just from the superwoman triathlon of children, home, and full-time job, but also a rare heart disease. As a young girl, at a time when the needed antibiotics weren't available, Mom suffered from rheumatic fever. This left her with a weakened heart and increased vulnerability to infection. Though she was healthy during my childhood, now that I was a teenager Mom was in and out of hospitals with a heart condition the doctors were unable to diagnose. She went through good and bad periods, but what was most excruciating for all of us was that no doctor could figure out Mom's illness. Consequently, there was no clear best way to treat her. No one in my family talked about how afraid we were of Mom's condition; we were experts at covering our feelings with too much doing. The free-spirited joie de vivre of my childhood had already turned into overachievement.

Though none of us, including my mother, discussed her condition, I knew she often suffered intensely. Very early one morning I got up to finish a term paper and found Mom pale as a ghost, pacing in her nightgown. Holding and rubbing her elbows and forearms, she said with desperation, "I've been up all night with this terrible pain in my arms. It feels like sharp needles. I've taken everything in the medicine closet and nothing helped."

"Will you have to go to the hospital again?" I asked, holding back my tears.

"I have no idea, absolutely no idea, and my damn doctors

don't either." Then she disappeared into the bathroom, leaving me alone with my terror and my unfinished term paper on Walt Whitman.

During my mother's frequent hospital visits Pop ran the house with elegant efficiency. Having learned to cook in the army, he chopped vegetables into giant piles of green, orange, red, and yellow, and then mixed them together for a salad big enough for twenty. Though he remained calm on the outside, I can barely imagine the enormous strain he felt inside. Once when Pop returned from a hospital visit he said to Jimmy, Joanie, and me, "Your mother's heart has grown too large. It has been working overtime." Only now do I appreciate the power of this precise graphic image: the shadow of the feminine, giving too much to others and not enough to the self.

Thankfully, there were comical parts to Mom's terrible disease. Unhealthy herself, she wanted her children to be in superb shape. Our mother became an early pioneer of health food, and soon strange things infiltrated our kitchen: wheat germ, molasses, yogurt, and, God forbid, whole wheat bread. Joanie and I used to sneak over to our neighbor Betsy Fleming's house to get our regular fix of white Wonder Bread. Turning us into unwilling guinea pigs for her "tiger's milk"—a horrendous mix of dark molasses, soy, and yogurt—our mother insisted this elixir could bring us long life. As my brother Jimmy said, "Mom was brilliant in finding ways to get me to unknowingly consume wheat germ. I often cursed Carlton Fredricks, as I never got to eat a normal waffle after she began to listen to him on the radio."

Looking back, I see how brave my mother was about both the terrible pain and the psychological strain of her illness. And even though so much of her physical and emotional vitality was dying, her essential self could still emerge. In her good periods she continued to be the life of any party. Special occasions at Tower Hill might find Mom sitting with a large sketch pad in her lap and a set of charcoals at her side. Lining up for her to draw their caricatures, the crowd would soon be in stitches as small noses became buttons, big noses hooks, chins doorknobs, dimples caverns, and eyebrows hedges of bushes. She was a genius with hair, turning curls into wild chaos and crew cuts into neatly mowed fields. Her impersonations were hilarious but never insulting. I cannot imagine my mother happier: surrounded by laughter, her fingers covered in black dust as she created small miracles across the smooth white page.

Mom loved to entertain at our house on Brecks Lane, and you could always hear her husky laugh above the din of conversation. I loved helping her fix the tray of Manhattans with the strong smell of bourbon and the bright red cherries in the slender-stemmed glasses. Slicing her favorite Wisconsin longhorn cheese and already slightly tipsy, my mother would say to me, "Darling, every woman has to know how to throw a great party. Mind you, not just a good party, but a great party." Indeed, I now have the reputation for throwing some of the best parties in the Hudson Valley. Once Mom's best friend Mary Jane Bird said to me in her wonderfully preserved southern accent, " Gail, your mother is a fabulous hostess. But it's really not just the parties, as much as that people just love being with your mom."

Only now, more than thirty years after her death, do I see how insidious and complex my mother's demons were. The combination of her perceived outsider status in Wilmington's high society, her heart disease, and her role as a working mother of three children all conspired to steal my mother's vital energy. Her rare heart condition was not just physical, but equally emotional and spiritual. I will never know which level of her disease was more profound, which caused her more suffering. Her heart was damaged by rheumatic fever and her heart was broken by the abandonment of her emotional intelligence and her interior compass. As her artist's intuition and imagination were slowly buried under family pressures and a growing need to keep up with society's standards, her inner life was swallowed whole by the dragon of outer demands. Back then I didn't know how precisely my mother's loss and broken heart mirrored the universal betrayal of the feminine in our society, nor could I begin to guess how much of my own life would be dedicated to making up for this loss, to battling with that very same ferocious dragon.

Inhabiting My Mother's Unlived Life

During my later high school years, as if by an unspoken pre-ordained agreement, I unconsciously began my lifelong pattern of inhabiting the life my mother wasn't living. The words of our silent secret pact read, "Daughter agrees to embody mother's real essence as long as mother forgets her authentic herself."

If she wanted to fit in with Wilmington's high society, then I would do the counterpoint, finding my place outside the bounds of a society I could never be part of. This was the early sixties and it wasn't just my home that was troubled and tumultuous, the world around me was also falling apart. President Kennedy had been assassinated, the civil rights movement was on fire, and though we didn't know it yet, the Vietnam War would be the end of America's innocence. Simultaneously rebelling against both my mother and high society's conservative values, I spent many of my weekends in Quaker work camps cleaning up neighborhoods and painting houses in the inner city of Philadelphia. Surrounded by passionate Quaker activists and African American community leaders, I could say with conviction to myself, and to Mom, I don't really care if I can't be part of high society.

During this time I experienced one of my first true love affairs—with Paula, a young black girl from Wilmington's inner city whom I tutored in reading every week for four years. When we met, I was fifteen and she was seven. Paula wore her hair in intricate braids wound with red ribbon, her skin was shiny ebony, and she had long skinny legs like me. She was sharp as a tack and as funny as anyone I had ever met. We sat close to one another on the tiny chairs at the low tables covered with red-checkered oilcloth in the basement of a local Baptist church. Our afternoons started with me helping Paula improve her reading. When she had had enough reading, the roles reversed.

"Come on now, Gail, I'm going to teach you how to dance the hully gully and the fish." And with the incomparable Supremes blasting "Stop! In the Name of Love," she did.

She also taught me the glorious Baptist hymns she sang every Sunday, and on occasion I would go to church with her family. Catholic mass was never the same after that. Paula can take much of the credit for my later telling the Peace Corps I would join only if they would send me to Africa, which they did.

Though I played the role of outsider with aplomb, there was a painful struggle going on inside me as well. Undoubtedly a reflection of my mother's ambiguity, some days I felt like the outsider who was hopelessly unrefined with the wrong clothes and no fancy vacations in Bermuda. Then I would become the other outsider, living on higher moral ground and making my own way, unlike my spoiled rich classmates. Back and forth my little drama swung between inferiority and superiority. Later, the archetype of the outsider would deeply inform my life's work as an empowerment guide and advocate for the disenfranchised. I became a worthy example of how a wounded place can heal into a great strength.

Mom supported my activities as a free spirit (her former self), so long as I also continued to look good in the eyes of Wilmington society (her new self), as editor of the school newspaper, secretary of the honor society, and captain of the lacrosse team. My split personality was reflected in my choice of friends, running the gamut from Wilmington debutantes to outsiders in the school, mostly students on scholarships or other teachers' children. Joanie played the role of rebel with gusto, smoking and drinking, hanging out with poets, and choosing boyfriends from the wrong side of the tracks. Jimmy took the leader role as the champion athlete and president of his class. As the middle kid I seemed to have straddled the worlds of both the in-group and out-group.

The clearer half of my distorted desire to prove myself as an outsider was my genuine fascination with diversity. When it was time to fill out the application for the American Field Service (AFS) Student Exchange Program, I told Mom that I absolutely had to get chosen. Somehow I understood this was the path for me, the direct route to happiness. At seventeen I already knew that I wanted to be part of a global family. Sure enough, I was soon acquiring my first passport and packing. As we sat on the edge of my bed with a large map of South America spread between us, my mother and I tried to make the connection between the red dot indicating my destination in Paraguay and the clothes I should pack for my first adventure in what would become a life of global travel. "The information packet says because it's below the Equator it's going to be winter there, not summer. But what does winter in South America mean? Oh, Mom, I don't have any idea what to bring." Completely overwhelmed, I collapsed on the one corner of the bed not buried under suitcases and literature on inoculations, how to purify drinking water, and things never to eat.

"Don't worry, sweetie," Mom replied with utter confidence. "I've already spoken to the AFS office in Washington and I found out that the weather will be like autumn here. It's your favorite season and I've picked out some of the outfits you love. And darling, I think you should wear your lovely quilted suit with pink roses on the plane to Buenos Aires. You want to look your best."

"No, Mom, it's too prissy. No way am I going to wear that. It's something you would wear!" My overwhelm turned ornery.

"Just try it on for me, and look in the mirror for yourself. If you don't feel really great you don't have to wear it." My mother had a great eye for clothes and she was patiently assisting my metamorphosis from tomboy into young woman.

I grabbed the quilted suit and yanked it over my head onto my long lanky body. Lo and behold, I did look lovely. I did look my best. "All right," I said begrudgingly, "I'll wear this on the plane. But Mom, what if no one else is this dressed up and I look different from everyone else?" My deepest vulnerability fully exposed, I started to cry. Though I was now taller than my mother, she tenderly took me in her arms and comforted me as if I were once again that small girl with a Dutch boy haircut and scrapes on her knees.

"I am so proud of you, sweetie," she whispered, her voice full of emotion. "The AFS committee knew what they were doing when they chose you. You are a natural leader and you're going to be a fine youth ambassador. This is your dream come true and it's normal that you are feeling nervous. Just be yourself, darling." With those simple words, my mother offered me the precise wisdom that I would need for the next four decades of my life.

Somehow we finished packing me up, and the next day the whole family went to see me off at the Philadelphia airport. Just before I got on the plane Mom handed me a box of airmail stationery that she'd already addressed. "So you can write to us about everything," she said, not even trying to stop the flow of tears down her cheeks.

"I will, Mom. Please, don't worry, I'm going to be fine. And I promise to write often," I said, embracing her, and sounding much braver than I felt. At the time I had no idea that Buenos Aires was to be the first in a series of final goodbyes to my mother. Mom knew, though, that with this first goodbye I was starting the process of making my own life outside of her house.

At seventeen into the fire I went, the first female AFS student sent to Paraguay. I spoke fair French but no Spanish and was totally unprepared for the cross-cultural differences I would confront. As my first in a lifetime of global ironies, I was sent to a small town in one of the poorest countries in the world and my AFS family was part of the wealthy upper class. "Now I am surrounded by Du Ponts who speak Spanish," I remember thinking. Considered a member of the family, I was assigned my own servant. Maria, only four years older than I was, ended up being my Spanish teacher, my friend, and my connection to the way most people in her country lived. Once we became friends, I joked with her, *"Maria, tu eres mi dama de honor."* Maria, you are my lady in waiting.

"Pero tu, Gail, eres mi estudiante de espanol," she would quickly respond. But you, Gail, you are my Spanish student.

As the first young woman AFS student in Paraguay, I required an adult chaperone whenever I left the house. I was also a lot taller than almost everyone in town and soon became quite a celebrity walking down the street towering above my chaperone. People felt no self-consciousness about studying me openly and with great curiosity. *Dios mio estas alta! Bonita, pero demasiada alta y flaca.* My height and skinny build was a topic of endless amazement and conversation.

My celebrity status included meeting the American ambassador and being interviewed for newspaper and radio. One newspaper article pictured me in a gaucho costume, astride a giant ostrich. Attending an astonishing number of receptions and teas in my honor, I became addicted to the strong maté tea that we drank through long silver straws. I loved being serenaded by handsome Latin men with guitars, and I exhilarated in the wild open Chaco countryside with its boisterous rodeos, but I was also terribly homesick for my family and Brecks Lane. On my senior page in the Tower Hill yearbook under "Mostly Likely Occupation," the caption reads, "Queen of Paraguay." Returning from Paraguay for my senior year at Tower Hill, I became the president of the AFS Club and proceeded to fall in love with Antonio from Madrid, Bjorn from Copenhagen, and Pacho from Rome. I was a shy teenager who dreaded the spin-the-bottle games and boys groping under my dress, but with my foreign brothers I was at home with myself and in love three times over.

Leaving the high school parties behind, the four of us found our way down to the Brandywine River, where a big old tire hung from a large oak. We twisted the swing's rope tightly so that it spun wildly as we swung way out over the dark waters of the Brandywine, whooping and hollering in four languages and finally plunging into the cold river. Shivering and ecstatic we climbed back onto the banks of the Brandywine, and Bjorn passed around his vodka flask to warm us up.

Meanwhile, this was also high season for Wilmington's debutante parties, and much like Sunday mass, my mother made absolutely certain that I attended as many of these extravaganzas as possible. Frankly, my most lasting memories of these important social occasions are the potent gin and tonics that gave all debutante parties a soft and diaphanous feeling in my mind. The biggest party that season was when Count Basie's Big Band played under a giant white tent. While the actual debutantes wore lovely pale pink and lavender, I chose a bright green chartreuse dress with a wide royal purple sash that Mom had helped me sew. I had also made big shiny chartreuse hoop earrings that perfectly matched my dress. By then, I was far too headstrong to allow my mother to persuade me to wear something more appropriately conservative. But that night it didn't matter that I would never fit in. That night I thought I had died and gone to heaven, so amazing was Count Basie's music soaring way out beyond the big white tent and touching the stars.

As I went off to college in September of 1967, my mother had exactly five years left to her life. A five-year period in which Martin Luther King and Robert Kennedy would be shot, and Vietnam and our ghettos would burn. What I didn't know then is that neither I, nor the world, would ever be the same after that time.

During those five years I was very rarely at home and then for only a week or two at a stretch. Meanwhile my mother grew more and more ill and I am now convinced that she probably knew she didn't have long to live. She was a fifty-year-old woman who wanted to live as fully as possible, who had patiently waited for her children to leave home so she could have time for herself and her art, yet she had an incurable heart disease. Those last years she graciously sent me off to college, to Paris, and finally to West Africa with her unspoken message, *Death is close by for me. You must go live fully.* And so I continued to inhabit my mother's unlived life.

PART TWO

Leaving My Mother's House

The Gradual Loss of the Feminine

I understand we are using up the very last minutes of something neither of us can call, outright, my childhood. I can't wait for you to leave, and then you do. I close the door and stand watching . . . And because no one can see me I wipe my slippery face with the back of my hand. My nose runs and I choke on tears, so many I am afraid I will drown. I can't smell the leaves or apples or woodsmoke at all. I feel more alone than I've ever felt in my life.

—Barbara Kingsolver, *Small Wonder*

The Final Years

At eighteen I thought I had forever with my mother. I didn't have a clue that these were our last years together, my only chance to know her woman to woman. Spanning the late sixties and early seventies, my college years found me a wild young thing completely unaware of anyone's fragile mortality. I was busy devouring life, engaging in nonviolent resistance against the Vietnam War, playing a leadership role at Skidmore College in the effort to shift the balance of power between students and faculty, and spending a raucous junior year abroad in Paris in 1968, where I studied Marxism while the student revolution was erupting all around. Then, right after college I went off to West Africa as a member of the Peace Corps.

My mother was extraordinarily understanding of my headlong adventures and my friends were often envious of the freedom she gave me. I wonder now, did my escapades remind her of her own untamed artist's life in her Denver loft? Or was it the darker presence of death on her shoulder that allowed my mother to grant me so much freedom, so much life? One incident stands out for me as a particularly strong symbol of

Mom's desire for me to have the freedom she knew I wanted. A few weeks before I left for Paris, she took me for a checkup with our beloved family physician, Dr. Mac.

After Mac had pronounced me fit as a fiddle, my mother casually mentioned that I'd won a full scholarship to go abroad for my junior year. "Gail's leaving for Paris soon and I know the change in climate might cause her monthly periods to be irregular," she said blandly, as if she were discussing the weather rather than her daughter's sexual freedom. "I'd like you to prescribe some birth control pills for her." And with that radical act of love from my devout Irish Catholic mother, I left Dr. Mac's with the round wheel of turquoise pills.

Indeed, I used the pills from the moment I left for Paris. My adventures started with a British rock-and-roll singer as we sailed from the harbor in New York City across the Atlantic to Calais on the S.S. *France.* I wore my white silk stockings and velvet green minidress up to my bottom, and dined in splendor on exquisite seven-course meals with my rock-and-roll man. After dinner, small cigars in hand, we would stroll the magnificent deck of the ocean liner debating the merits of British and American rock stars.

In Paris I would have an international mix of lovers— French, Vietnamese, Haitian, and Canadian. (Yes, those were the days long before AIDS.) François, Jean Louis, Ernest, and Barry were all part of my sexual awakening as well as my global education. François was a passionate Marxist deeply involved with the French student revolution who taught me more about communism than my classes at the Sorbonne. He carefully explained that at the core of Marxism was the idea that we must look at the world as a whole in relation to each of its parts. Since formal religions were now collapsing, Marxism was an attempt at a world ethic. Jean Louis was a poet, the first Vietnamese I had ever met, and he brought great subtlety and complexity to our heated discussions about the

Vietnam War. Ernest was an exotically handsome refugee from Haiti who offered me my first heartbreaking lessons about political prisoners and leaving one's family far behind. And Barry, my Canadian lover, taught me about French cabaret, Ionesco, and most especially about drugs.

More memorable than those flings, though, was the way I fell in love with Paris. I explored the city on foot, wearing my long khaki hippie coat down to my ankles and my long hippie hair down to my waist. I fed my voracious cultural appetite with ten-hour days of museums, concerts, cathedrals, and gardens. On countless afternoons I sat in the Jeu de Paume and the Rodin sculpture garden, mesmerized by the beauty and the ever-changing human parade. I spent hours in the Bois de Boulogne reading Baudelaire and Proust and writing in my journal. I had my favorite patisserie where Madame LeBrun knew me by first name. "Bonjour, Mademoiselle Gail, comment ça va aujourd'hui? Attends un petit moment et je vous donne votre café au lait avec beaucoup de lait, et votre pâtisserie chocolat." She knew exactly which dark chocolate pastry I loved and the way I took my café au lait extra light every day.

I wrote long letters to my parents during that year in France. It was Mom who really treasured these letters, keeping them all in the wooden box carved with her initials that Pop had helped me make for her. I still have those letters in that simple pine box with JWS so carefully carved on the top. Here my twenty-year-old self tries to explain Paris to my parents.

Dear Mom and Pop,

I am still ecstatic about Paris. I discover new and more amazing treasures everyday. The opera costs 80 cents and a Bach concert in a 15th century church costs $1.50—fantastic! I spend a lot of time at the Louvre

Museum. I love the guides at the Louvre—I wish I could look like them and talk like them. Today I went with my friend François for a picnic in the Bois de Boulogne. We ate baguette and five kinds of French cheese and lovely red wine. Then we went boating on a beautiful lake, all like a scene from a Monet painting, Mom. I feel so at home in Paris perhaps because so many wonderful and sad things have happened to me here.

If only I could describe to you why I love Paris. It's so many sided, it sings, it laughs, it yells and fights, and just throbs with life. There's a kind of unified diversity, a delightful stubbornness. There's so much pride, old wisdom along with an eternally young spirit. It's so elegant, so French, and so impossibly different than me, an American. Everywhere is such intricate finely composed beauty. More than anything it's this beauty that has captured me.

When I read this letter now I desperately want to rewrite my story and have it be my mother who lived that year in France. I want to know how she felt poring over these letters, brimming with my innocent wonder. I want to believe that when she read these letters from her daughter she could see herself in every word. I want somehow to give her my life, just hand it to her and say, "Live, please live, my dearest mother. If only it could have been you who had all those blessed hours in the Louvre and the Jeu de Paume. It was you who was the artist. You who loved color, shape, and light, and who never missed an opportunity to point those things out to me. It was you who taught me to appreciate beauty as a way to stay sane."

My year abroad ended with the quintessential hitchhiker's journey through the Greek Islands and Morocco. I was a poster girl for the hippie era, living in the caves on

Crete, then with a wealthy French doctor in his villa on Rhodes, and on to the mysterious marketplaces of Fez and the rooftop civilization in Marrakech, where our primary diet consisted of hashish. My insatiable cultural curiosity was satisfied by every aspect of these adventures, lively conversations with the people, enjoying the culinary and artistic pleasures, and taking in the splendid landscapes on foot. Spawned by my outsider status, my love of diversity was now blossoming into its opposite, where I felt like I belonged anywhere in the world.

Probably more worldly after my year of exuberant freedom, surely I was still innocent and unaware of the darker forces that enter every life. My naïve freedom was in perfect contrast with the angel of death on my mother's shoulder. When I returned to Brecks Lane, I had barely a few weeks for Mom to help me get ready for my senior year at Skidmore. The fury of my activity was fueled by a potent combination of being a self-centered twenty-year-old overachiever and my deeply hidden fear of Mom's illness. This collusion kept me far away from my mother's house, those rooms of unfulfilled dreams and impending death.

Decades later, my acute feeling that death was constantly close by for me was a distorted way for me to make up for these years of selfishness. It was as if I believed on some level that being close to lady death would somehow bring me close to my mother, as if by understanding death I could finally understand the depths of my mother's psyche in her final years. How very different my life would have been if Mom had discussed her feelings and fears about her illness and mortality. In trying to protect me from death, in pretending that the dark presence hadn't already filled our house, she had in fact instilled an unnatural terror in me. But she had already slammed the doors on the rooms of her heart; those rooms where our innermost feelings are cherished, where exposing fear is the highest kind of courage, where the mysteries of death are explored with open wonder, where we rest in the comfort of knowing that love outlives death. In those days no one else around her kept these doors open, so why would she? Even today, how often are you and I brave enough to open these doors wide and welcome all the unexpected and unruly visitors who tend to visit the chambers of the heart? After all, it is so much safer in the rooms of the head, where the visitors are rational and capable of controlling things. Can you blame Mother?

Returning to college in 1970, I was as far away from my feelings and any curiosity about death as a person could be. The Vietnam War was raging, and as a political science major I became deeply involved with the Quaker nonviolent resistance movement. I learned to train others in nonviolence and we were forever bonded through the holy trinity of sit-ins, protest songs, and tear gas. Profoundly politicized by my Marxist friends in Paris, I chose as a senior thesis the organizing and running of a food co-op to serve the poor in downtown Saratoga Springs. My thesis advisor, a gifted professor and sixties radical, helped me buy an old yellow school bus that had been cut in half and made into a strange-looking truck. We used Old Yellow to pick up large crates of fresh fruit and vegetables at the Albany farmer's market. Consistent with my inclusive "room for everything and everyone" approach, I would come home from the food co-op and change from my work shirt and jeans into the elegant, sophisticated clothes I wore for the modeling job that helped me pay my college tuition.

Living off campus, I was caretaker for the house of one of the principals for the New York City Ballet. Michael introduced me to both the world of dance and the world of gay men. He knew I was a hard worker and once brought me along to help paint the prima ballerina Suzanne Farrell's new country home. Michael and I grew enormously fond of each other, and he insisted that I attend his rehearsals because this was the best way to learn about ballet. Many afternoons, I would drive Old Yellow over to the Saratoga Performing Arts Center and watch transfixed as George Balanchine guided his company through hours of grueling practice. Balanchine's inspiring genius forever impressed on me the partnership between sweat and tears and seemingly effortless grace.

In spite of the fact that I was in free-spirit mode, I managed to graduate with honors, to my parents' enormous relief. A month after graduation I was off to the Peace Corps training camp in the Virgin Islands. Mom didn't have long, but our unspoken agreement was in full force as I lived with enough intensity for both of us. Of course if I could turn back time, I would have slowed down and turned inward and towards my mother. Instead, I was faster and more outward directed than ever. The more my mother left behind her interior female wisdom, the more I embraced outer masculine accomplishment. The closer my mother came to her death, the further away I went.

Mother Africa

My Peace Corps assignment took me to West Africa, a place that will, for me, be forever linked with my mother's death. On my first trip to Africa, Mom was ostensibly in reasonably good health. My first flight back to the States was a sudden trip home for her open-heart surgery, the second flight back was a devastating and unexpected return for her funeral, and on the last trip back I returned home to Brecks Lane a confused young woman with a closed heart. Those long trips across continents and oceans from New York City to Abidjan etched long lines in my psyche about innocence and its loss.

While my mother was battling a rare heart condition, I was falling under the spell of Africa's heart—her vivid colors and textures, her jubilant music and dance, her marvelous chaos and spontaneity, and most of all the warmth of the African people. With her generous heart, Africa mothered me even as I lost my own mother. Thinking about how surrounded I was by vitality in the last year of my mother's life, I am once again struck by the way the opposites stretched between us. Is it because she died during this time that more than thirty years later my years in Africa remain so alive?

As I had in Paris, I wrote often to my parents describing my life in West Africa. Scrawled in my unique and horrendous handwriting, my letters and brightly colored postcards were all saved in my mother's wooden JWS box. It was always Mom who responded, not Pop, telling me how much she loved my mail and that she often brought my letters to work at Stockwell's Antiques, where she read aloud my lively musings to the people she worked with. I imagine her sitting at the lunch table at the well-known Wilmington antiquary, saying to her colleagues, "I have some new letters from Gail over in Africa. As usual she's having more adventures than I can keep up with. I love the way she describes things, but lordy I wish her handwriting were easier to read."

October 1971

Dear Mom and Pop,

Mom, you asked me to describe a typical day and how I feel living in Africa. Here's a description from my journal that I like.

Africa, shortly after dawn the deep orange symmetry of the sun burns away the soft mist that touches down like angel hair on the straw huts, and grass, and dusty roads. By noon all is starched and stiffened by the fierce heat of the sun. Stark white butterflies light in the freshness of red velvet hibiscus. Stillness everywhere, even the lizards. Inside is the welcome coolness of bare stone floors. Quiet breezes come in from the giant mango trees always to coax me asleep for siesta. And at evening all is alive again. Graceful women veiled in pastel yellow, pink, blue, and white, walk home from prayers at the mosque. Children sing and cry. Young boys play soccer to the tune of drums. Rice and spicy peanut sauce scent the dusk air. A silent sun sets behind mountain clouds.

Africa, those moments when my rhythm is to sing and dance with you in the sun—softly, joyously, spontaneously—how I love you then! But when my other side—order, discipline, and structure—strains against your natural rhythm, we seem so foreign to one another then.

February 1972

Dear Mom and Pop,

I am on a train crossing the savannah on my way to Dakar, Senegal. Trains, African trains, an experience never to be forgotten. Everyone and everything piled into one car. Hens, goats, and cows too! The train stops every twenty minutes or so. Then, piled high on their heads, beautiful young African girls bring water, peanuts, tomatoes, coconuts, bananas, mangoes, papayas, guavas, colas, and strange looking meat and fish to the windows of the train. And everyone, including the animals, dives in pandemonium towards the windows to buy the food. Later, eating a mango, I sit with my feet hanging out the side of the train watching the grass huts and savannah go by with the soft breeze keeping me cool.

Soon we have to stop on an animal preserve to fix the smoking train engine. Mon Dieu, il fait chaud! (My God, it's hot!) The kind of heat that leaves your mouth and nose parched no matter how much water you drink. Roosters crow, tiny streaks of wind, and everything else still, dusty, dry, so still. Here the mud huts are soft and round built on flat grassy lands. Drums beat all night

long. We see elephant tracks, buffalo dung, green monkeys, cobras, and water holes in the high rust colored
grass.

The warmth and spontaneous generosity of my African
friends made a lasting impression on me. I have rarely en-
countered such hospitality. Though most of them lived very
simply, I always had the feeling of abundance when I was
with them. It was these Muslim friends who introduced me to
Islam. I loved waking every morning to the ancient sound of
the prayer call floating over my small village and welcoming
us to a new day. On Muslim holy days I attended services in
the red clay mosque wearing my veil of pastel blue. Enveloped
by the sound of whispered prayers, I felt comforted in the same
way as I was by the Latin prayers from my Catholic youth.
This experience made it all the more heartbreaking for me
when, thirty years later, post-9/11, I watched the American
media lump all Muslims together as potential terrorists. Such
crude thinking would be as preposterous as if during the period when I was in Africa, post-1963 and -1968, my African
friends had categorized me as a potential assassin. Today, if
one of my Muslim friends in New York invites me to celebrate
Ramadan I graciously accept, remembering my first Ramadan
feast in a mosque on the African savannah.

April 1972

Dear Mom and Pop,

I have told you that many of my African friends are
Muslims. This week is Ramadan feast, the most glorious of all Muslim celebrations, and yesterday I wrote
this little passage about Ramadan.

Feast, glorious Ramadan feast!
Prayers murmur devout whispers.
The mosque is a wave of pastel colored robes as
　you bow to Allah.
And then you people are joyous with your love
　of God and life.
Your feast and dance are jubilant.
Balafoons and drums beat and sing all the night.
Even as dawn comes, mist and shadows, your
　delight and celebration continue.
In Ramadan is the African spirit, a pure transcen-
　dent joy.
An inexplicable love of life.

My time in Africa was both holy and hilarious, though I tended to describe only the holy in my letters home. Shortly after I arrived at my Peace Corps post I was given a heavy red Honda motorcycle. At five feet, eight inches tall, I weighed 120 pounds and I could barely lift the kickstand. Riding over the treacherous sandy roads through the untamed African savannah I fell off the motorcycle more than I stayed on. Once I skidded in the sand and the bike fell so hard on my thigh that I can still rub the permanent dent in my leg.

My legs were so full of cuts and bruises that the nurses at the infirmary would greet me with a cheery, "Mon Dieu, qu'est-ce qui se passe aujourd'hui, Mademoiselle Catastrophe?" *My God, what has happened to you today, Miss Catastrophe?*

One fine afternoon I went to get my long hippie hair cut by an African barber. I was not yet fluent in the local dialect and communication was garbled. I left the barbershop with a Marine crew cut. My friends graciously told me I looked less American and more African with my shorn locks. Once I got over the shock, I realized it was much cooler that way.

While in Africa I fell in love with teaching and took the first steps toward my life's work. My mentor was Nora Hodges, a legend in the Peace Corps. In her early seventies, tiny and slightly humpbacked, Nora dressed exquisitely in the vibrant African tie-dyed material with intricate embroidery along the neck. She seemed to consist of pure energy, a veritable whirlwind of charisma who left me breathless and inspired.

Nora, or Madame Hodges as we were to call her, taught the Peace Corps volunteers TEFL—teaching English as a second language. With the TEFL method, we spoke only English in the classroom and used as varied a vocabulary as possible. Most of my students were gifted in languages, already fluent in French as well as several tribal dialects. For fun I gave my students African American names, mostly those of contemporary artists and athletes.

Sometimes Madame Hodges would observe us teaching so that she could give feedback and direction. One typical school day I didn't know that she was observing me from outside my classroom window, and that a video camera was rolling. Starting at 6:30 in the morning to avoid the fierce African sun, my first class of fifty students was chatting away in a myriad of dialects when I arrived. Immediately we switched to English.

"Wilson Pickett, how are you this morning?" I greeted one of my students.

"Very well thank you, Miss Straub," my student replied with a perfect American accent.

"How did you get to school this morning, Mr. Pickett?"

"I walked to school with my sister, but I would like to have your red motorcycle." I blushed, and raucous laughter ensued in the classroom. All my students knew of my unfortunate exploits on the Honda. Indeed, that very morning my knees were wrapped in bandages. Avoiding further embarrassment, I quickly engaged another student. "And Mr. James Brown, how are you this morning? What did you have for breakfast?"

"I am very well, Miss Straub. I had rice and sauce for breakfast," said Kofi, who had asked for his American name given his fondness for the singer. My sister, Joanie, who worshipped James Brown, had sent me magazine photos of the soulful man that I gave to the elated Kofi. "And did you cook your breakfast, Mr. Brown?" Again, raucous laughter.

"No, no, Miss Straub, in Africa a man does not cook his breakfast." Though Kofi's English was still flawless, he was clearly dismayed by my question.

"And why is that, Mr. James Brown?" I continued, more focused on the rich vocabulary my student was demonstrating than the fact that I had challenged his entire worldview. "I don't know Miss, it's just the way it is." Shouting began and many hands went up to answer the question. By now James Brown had abandoned the English language and he was defending himself in animated African dialect.

Later Nora took me aside. In her firm but irresistible way, she let me know that I should never have asked Kofi if he cooked his breakfast. "You know very well how it is in Africa, Gail. Your cross-cultural training covered this in great detail." Her penetrating eyes bore right into me. "But," her gaze softened, "I must say you are a natural. You have the makings of a master teacher. Keep practicing, young lady."

My Peace Corps experience continued to unfold and open up my life in new ways. I was surrounded by the sensual and emotional vitality of a people who lived in their bodies and close to their feelings. Mother Africa had kept the doors of her heart open, reminding me that not all places in the world placed the intellect over emotion, or the rational mind over the sensual joy of the body. This great mother continent was imprinting me with the feelings and sensations that many years later would save me.

My bouts of loneliness and homesickness were a small price to pay for my rich love of Africa. The cultural differences, from something as simple as the food to the complexity of being one of a handful of white people in my town, challenged me and forever changed my assumptions. Though this was the third foreign culture I had lived in, it was in West Africa where I faced the fact that my own country was made up of equal parts light and shadow. I would never again view America as the benign center of the universe, but rather as a country with positive and negative aspects that needed to coexist as part of a much larger global community. In the coming years this understanding would deeply inform who I was and the choices I made.

Then one day everything changed. I had been in Africa for a little over a year when the doctors finally decided that the only way to save Mom was to perform what was at that time highly experimental open-heart surgery. I went home immediately for the risky operation. That visit home was the last time I would see my mother alive, and it is a blur of excruciating memories.

By the time I reached the hospital in Philadelphia I was suffering from both jet lag and intense culture shock. I had been living mostly in the open air surrounded by the sweet smells of mango and banana trees, and now a nurse was leading me down a long, sterile hospital corridor full of the bitter smells of pain and sickness. Mom lay in a special unit of intensive care. I hadn't seen her in over a year, and here she was bruised and unconscious with tubes everywhere, looking as if she had already died. So deep and lasting was my horror at this sight that even today when I enter a hospital I have to fight off nausea. Even today I have an inordinate fear of illness.

My brave mother made it through her surgery and returned home. Both Jimmy and Joanie were married by then, and they were back at Brecks Lane with their spouses. Joanie's baby son Jake was Mom's healing inspiration. She used to call her grandson Little Lachie, her shortened version of his middle name

Lachlan. One of Joanie's last memories of our mother was of her watching Jake. He was standing at the edge of the sofa where Mom was resting. She looked at him with great tenderness. "Look at you, Little Lachie, you're only ten months old and you're already walking. I want to get better so I can pick you up and hug you." I remember distinctly a moment when Joanie gave Jake a piece of soft licorice, perhaps for teething, and as the black drool spread all over Little Lachie's face, my mother's husky laugh touched all of us. It was one of the last times that this heart-warming sound would fill our Brecks Lane house.

Mom's recovery took place in early summer and she would rest on the chaise lounge out in the soft warm light of her beloved garden. She was fragile but cheerful. In one of my final conversations with her just before I left to return to West Africa, we sat together among her snapdragons, petunias, and zinnias. My mother didn't speak of death or fear or sadness; she wanted to hear about my life thousands of miles away. Always the one to shed light on others, Mom's love was like the diffuse warm glow that emanated from the garden we sat in.

Mom had on her favorite comfortable turquoise green muumuu, and she was enjoying the fresh clear day. "So tell me, sweetie, how are your students? And didn't you say you had traveled by boat to Nigeria? That must have been exciting. And darling, you are still taking your malaria medicine regularly aren't you? You look a little too thin." She spoke as if we had forever.

These were my last precious moments basking in my mother's generous presence. No matter how hard I wrack my brain, I can't remember my final responses to my mother. I fear the profound shame at my unawareness will forever block those words. If there was a single week in my life I could change it would be that final one with my mother. How could I not have seen how close to death she was? Why didn't I ask her to tell me the story of her life, her joys and sorrows, her triumphs and regrets? How could I possibly have gone back to my Peace Corps service? (Of course it was she who insisted that I do.) How could I have been so stupid, so selfish, such an utter failure as a daughter? Could I ever have been so young?

Several months after my return to Africa I was in my house one morning when I suddenly got violently ill. I was shaken to the core with gut-wrenching vomiting. The German doctor could find no cause so he sent me home to rest. Just a few hours later a message came that I was to go see the headmaster of the school where I was teaching. News traveled fast in our small town, so I thought maybe he had heard that I wasn't feeling well and wanted to check up on me. "Entrez, Mademoiselle Gail. Assiez vous, assiez vous." There was a long pause, as the elegant African headmaster looked out the window searching for the right words, and then he turned to me and said very gently, "Votre mère est mort." *Your mother is dead.* Yes, my violent illness had occurred at the precise time of my mother's death.

To get to Mom's funeral I had to travel more than ten hours over rough dirt roads in the African open-air buses that teemed with people, mangoes, yams, chickens, and goats. By the time I arrived at the airport I was caked in the red dirt from the roads. It filled my nostrils, ears, eyelids—my entire body was encased in red earth. Then, once again, I took the fourteen-hour plane ride home. By the time I reached Brecks Lane I was numb and exhausted, but I pretended to be strong as I had always done all through my mother's unraveling.

The only things I remember from my mother's funeral were that I wore a midnight blue dress with hand-embroidered flowers and that Mom's plot in the cemetery seemed so lonely, as if she had arrived far too early in her resting place. It was an Indian summer day, achingly beautiful with yellow leaves against a clear blue sky. Our funeral procession of long black cars with tinted windows passed all the other gravestones, and we laid Mom to rest in a plot all by herself; just my mother in the fresh brown earth with the cloudless azure sky above her.

The day after she was buried I went through Mom's closet. In the front were the conservative plaid suits she wore to work, her silk blouses thick with the scent of Christian Dior perfume, and her beloved party dresses. Way in the back, neatly out of view but never discarded, were the more colorful artistic clothes she had abandoned many years earlier. There, suspended on hangers, was a review of my mother's life, her style and taste, her moods and ambiguities, her hopes and dreams. But that day I was far too numb and afraid to feel any of part of her. I boxed up my grief as I boxed up her clothes. Numbly, I sent everything off to Aunt Mae and our Colorado cousins. This numbness went on for years. For years it was if the red earth from the road that carried me to her funeral encased my unspeakable grief.

After the funeral my father insisted that I return to Africa rather than stay home with him. So I left my home on Brecks Lane and I left my mother's house forever. I left the house where her presence had shaped me and I entered a place where my mother's absence would now inform who I was.

Crossing the Sahara
Closing My Heart

During the final months of my Peace Corps service I went through the motions of my life as if I were deep underwater. No sound, smell, or illumination penetrated the liquid that seemed to surround me, isolating me from feeling anything. When it was time to leave Africa, though not fully aware of the spiritual implications, I chose to make a pilgrimage across the Sahara Desert with a group of Tuareg nomads and their camel caravan. But rather than awaken me, helping to reveal the truth, in the end this pilgrimage achieved the opposite, deadening my heart, hiding what was real. As I traversed the Sahara and left behind the warm open heart of Mother Africa, I made an unspoken decision to bury my grief. Somewhere in the vast stretches of sand, I crossed an invisible line back into the territory of rational thinking, mind over heart, doing over feeling, animus over anima. In the vast stretches of sand I thought I could erase all traces of the wisdom that a mother passes down to a daughter.

The phases of my pilgrimage across the great desert reflected my internal shifting. Starting in Agadez, Niger, I made preparations for my two-month journey north into Algeria and the stark Hoggar Mountain Range. A small paradise of artistry, the Agadez market was vibrant with Tuareg women weaving intricate straw mats and designing bright leather camel saddles. They sat on the ground, silent and reverent as if praying, embroidering fine black and white desert clothes that were open and fluid, so that when the desert wind blew the air would cool the body. Throwing silver into sand pits glowing orange from the hot coals, Tuareg silversmiths forged splendid crosses, bracelets, and boxes. Camels were everywhere.

Soon, I was given my desert clothes, a long sheer black robe and a high black turban that covered my face and head against the relentless Sahara sun. Teaching me how to carefully wrap my turban, an old Tuareg woman explained how these folds would stay in place and shield me when the strong winds came. When dressed, I felt both light and closed in; only my eyes peaked out from a tiny slit in my turban. Then, I experienced the legendary Bedouin generosity as she offered me a beautiful old silver Tuareg cross as protection in the Sahara.

Regal beyond description, the Tuareg women stood over six feet tall. Gliding across the desert with their long robes and flowing folds, great turbans of white, black, and indigo blue, they seemed to float just above the sand as if they were mirages. In every regard the women nomads were equal to men, unheard of in most of Africa. They controlled all mediums of magic and medicine, and used intricate herbal formulas for birth control. Trance dancing was common, and the men were thought to be much more susceptible to evil spirits. Only the Tuareg women were capable of driving away the demons. The sisters were also the masters of poetry and music.

Mesmerized by the Bedouin women, I felt as if I had entered an advanced realm of the sacred feminine. Powerful and mysterious, this feminine connected me to my mother's essence for a final time before I would shut tight my heart, leaving my female lineage in the desolate towering sand dunes. The Tuareg women, with all their instinctual wisdom, spirituality, and artistry, reminded me of what Mom had given me before she left herself. Here in the great desert, women's intuition was held in the highest regard, understood as a guiding light in the most important affairs of life. The invisible, inexplicable, and irrational were revered as aspects of the mystical. The inner world of the imagination where poetry, music, art, and dreams were cultivated was an essential equal partner to the outer world of commerce and government. Here in Agadez, as in my childhood, my mother would have been at home with herself as artist, mystic, and wise woman.

Surrounded by such loveliness, I met Bello, a photographer from *National Geographic*. Dressed in my sheer black desert robe, I asked him, "What on earth are you doing in Agadez?"

"You mean you don't know?" he replied, astonished. "There's an extremely rare total eclipse of the sun near Hoggar, in the Sahara. I've come to photograph it."

"No, no, I don't know anything. I'm just on my way home," I replied as if I made this trip all the time, forgetting he didn't know that I had spent two years living in West Africa and I was just finding my way back to Europe via the desert.

"You're what!" Bello laughed, and flirted with me. "On your way home by crossing the Sahara Desert! What kind of creature are you?"

Soon we were on our camels with our goatskins full of water slung by our sides, crossing miles of sand, heading into the towering mountains of the Mouydir. The dark peaks seemed to spring out of nowhere, ragged and *découpée*, unearthly as if we had landed on the moon. Penetrating black presences against the vast stretches of white, they beckoned in an irrefutable way. There was no green anywhere except when we came upon an oasis, each one a heavenly little womb in the middle of the stark terrain. Stunning in their contrast, the lush oases are breathtakingly beautiful, replete with waterfalls, mints, dates, figs, oranges, and lemons.

Magenta orchid bushes flooded the sides of the streams, giving the illusion that the water was on fire. In the evening we drank strong smoky tea as we lay cradled in the sand under stars so close they seemed to stroke us. Time as we knew it had disappeared into this vast space. Long into the night, the Tuaregs recited stories and poetry in their complex language filled with images of camel caravans, desert plants, sand storms, and lovers embracing.

After a week of the bumping rhythm on camelback we arrived in the Hoggar, and Bello prepared to photograph the total eclipse. He had brought an astonishing array of cameras and telescopic lenses into the Sahara. Existing in profound harmony with the earth, the Tuaregs were curious but fearful about the fact that the sun would be completely blackened in the middle of the day. The nomads wondered aloud how the camels and small desert creatures would respond to the noonday darkness. The day itself was slightly overcast, not what Bello had hoped for. An hour before the eclipse, the entire caravan gathered together and silently awaited the coming miracle. As the dark slowly, inexorably takes over the light, a hushed and eerie quiet filled the already motionless Sahara. No one spoke or moved as the inexplicable unfolded, changing us all in invisible ways.

Later that evening, as the darkness we were accustomed to approached, there was a momentous celebration in our camp. Amidst the peaks of the Hoggar, the high shrill tone of the women's voices pierced the stillness. The sound of the calabash, a large gourd filled with water and played like a string instrument, was as glorious as any Bach cello suite. Bello and I both wept from the sheer force of the nomads' music bursting out into the immensity of the Sahara. That night I felt a sadness too large to name. Yes, Bello was leaving tomorrow, and I would no longer be traveling with my beloved Tuaregs, as now an Algerian guide would take me the rest of the way across the desert by truck. But it was much more, this sadness. I think now that the haunting desert music that night was a funeral dirge for my mother. The Tuaregs' song touched me so deeply it was as if they had sung of a mother's death too young, and her lost daughter headed for a home that could no longer be called home. The symbol of the total eclipse hiding the sun could not have been more prescient for the coming years of my life, in which my denial would eclipse the true light of my being.

And so, I left a people and a place where the artistic, the spiritual, and the sensual were the closest of sisters; where the natural world was integrated into every aspect of the sacred; and where intuition was so highly regarded that most people could sense the presence of people and events long before they took place. I came out of this holy place into Northern Algeria, the transition phase of my journey. Walking through the cobbled streets shaded by date and palm trees, I met women dressed in white robes, fully veiled, with only a tiny eye peering through at the world. If only I had recognized it, I would have seen it as yet another visual allegory for my emotional state. Making my way through the narrow and crooked streets, I arrived at the Moorish baths, which provided blessed relief for my tired body unaccustomed to the days on camelback. Later I was invited by my guide to take tea and hear the children sing their lessons from the Koran.

Then suddenly, the final phase of my pilgrimage was upon me. I arrived in Marseilles after two months in the desert and two years in West Africa. Nothing could have prepared me for the shock: efficiency, efficiency, banks and money, everyone rushing everywhere. Fat people, no one smiled. Old French women stared at me. Now I was on the train going to Paris, tiny cabins, windows shut, doors shut, people shut. All around were constipated clothes and conversation. My heart was bursting. I could not put into words the sadness I felt in leaving Africa; her profound humaneness and gay nonchalance, her sun and sensual gracefulness, her freedom of spirit. I would always love her. Mother Africa and my mother were now indistinguishable, my poignant goodbye to the continent the singular way I could fathom a goodbye to Mom.

Leaving Africa's warm maternal love, taking off my black desert clothes and the silver cross for protection, I was lost. Adrift in my life, I was not sure what I would do next. What I had known as my family and my home would never be the same. Now culture shock and the shock of my mother's death crashed down on my heart and closed it tight. I had lost my mother, the person who had always tried to understand how I felt, the person who could best help me navigate my own inner landscape. This woman whom I had fully taken for granted, who had lighted the rooms of my life, was gone. Now I was trapped in those dark and lonely rooms where I would try to keep feelings at bay, doing everything by myself. Both I and the culture that I was returning to had lost our mothers, the guardians of the interior.

The Death of My Family

Motherless daughters talk about empty spaces.
They talk about missing pieces. They talk about
the void that exists where a family once was, and
the gaping hole that sits permanently between
their stomach and their ribs.
—Hope Edelman, *Motherless Daughters*

After the Sahara I returned home to Brecks Lane for a short
time before I moved to Boston. Everything, from the big things
to the smallest details, was utterly different without my mother.
Mom was the glue that held our family together and without
her we were loving but separate pieces that never really came
together again. As the literal symbol of the death of our family, our beloved dog Rocky died just weeks after my mother
passed away.

We tried to carry on the rituals of holidays, all of us eating at the long Shaker dining room table that Pop had made
for Mom. Jimmy and Joanie would come home with their families for these occasions. My nephew Jake was soon joined by

another redhead, his cousin Jason, who was Jimmy's firstborn son. There was no better tonic for my father than to be around his grandsons. Joanie and I would make the table lovely with bright fresh flowers, the white damask table cloth, and our mother's best silver and china, as she had taught us so well. But it could never be the same without her; the spark of our family had gone out. Mom was the one who kept us in touch by communicating our news back and forth, who helped us understand the intrinsic patterns of our lives, the one who made sure we honored the eternal through the celebration of traditions. As she had sorted our childhood clothes and toys, later she helped us sort the interior contents of our lives, our dreams and our confusions. Her ineffable presence wove us together through the loom of her emotional depth, her spirituality, and her love of beauty. This invisible yet essential feminine presence, this veritable life force that has been so undervalued in our world, was what connected us and made us a family. Is it only when something is gone that we can value all that it is? I pray that this isn't so.

After his shattered family left, Pop was so brave and so heartbroken. Living with him now in the home he and my mother had so lovingly created was his lineage of loss: his own father's suicide when Pop was twelve, the dire poverty he grew up with, his sister's untimely death, tending my mother during all the years of her mysterious heart ailment, and now her death just when the two of them could have enjoyed life together without the responsibility of three children. But this lineage of loss is not the only thing that stays with me about my father. What also lingers is my father's spacious intelligence and the way all kinds of people felt at home with him, as if the loss had carved a space in him large and generous enough to hold everyone. I don't know where my father's strength came from, but sometimes I feel it running through me like a river whose sure current reminds me of how resilient the human spirit can be. Much later in my life and years after Pop had died, when my work put me in intimate contact with immigrant women who had had survived genocide and war, their resiliency brought my father close to me again.

My father did his best to guide his lost daughter. Like most men of his generation, feelings were *verboten,* so his direction was focused on the outer aspects of my life: where I would live and how I would make my living. Since we had never spoken of inner things, we had no trail into that territory now. Our intimacy was firmly grounded in our mutual love of world affairs, but we were strangers in the land of the interior. I was relieved and happy when Pop remarried and enjoyed the companionship of Evelyn for some years before he died in 1987. An executive at a hospital, and ultraconservative by my standards, Evelyn was very different from Mother. But I grew fond of her just because she took such tender care of Pop. On the weekend my father was getting married I came down with a fever of 103, later diagnosed as malaria, which had stayed in my bloodstream from Africa. I was too sick to attend his wedding and thus, yet again, I had the perfect excuse not to face my untouched grief.

Settled into the rhythm of their lives, both Jimmy and Joanie now had their own families to anchor them. Over the years Jimmy adopted his wife Patti's loving parents, this family becoming the center of his life. In the following decades Joanie and I would build a precious and lasting friendship, for me all that remains of our family. My mother's presence held us together, and without her my origins were scattered all around me. I began my lifelong pursuit of replacing the Straub family with a wide range of creative substitutes, including a hippie commune, a decades-long women's group, the global family, and ultimately a real and lasting community in Woodstock, New York, where I eventually settled. Years later, my life's work would be involved with creating spiritual families for those who were orphaned from their roots in a variety of ways. Again my own story of loss seemed a direct reflection of the larger culture, which had lost the conscious feminine, guardian of relationships, family, and community. In the coming years hundreds of spiritual orphans would come to my retreats in search of family, a safe place away from the incessant demands of outer life, a supportive community where they could examine the interior contents of their lives.

But in those years of my early twenties there were no such retreats. I was completely afloat, not sure which culture I belonged to, not sure what I was to do with my life, not sure of anything. I needed someone to calibrate my interior compass, to show me how to pay attention and how to read its signals. I needed a mother.

The Pumpkin House
Second Childhood

Returning from Africa in 1973 lost and confused, I blended right in with the rest of the world dazed by Nixon and Watergate, Vietnam and the killing fields in Cambodia. With so much injustice and death all around, the hippie movement was a last fling with innocence, the baby boomer's refusal to grow up, a creative attempt to camouflage reality with free love, rock and roll, and drugs. I, too, desperately needed to find a way to numb the pain and death inside me. Indeed you could say that being a hippie was just about custom made for me at this time in my life. These next years were also my last hurrah with innocence, my naïve attempt to run away from my suffering. Yes, these were highly creative years and, yes, sooner or later like the rest of my generation I would have to grow up. But please, not yet!

My first experiment in creating a new family took place in the Pumpkin House, a full-fledged hippie commune on Boston's North Shore. My confusion transparent, I entered a wild and doomed relationship with a man seventeen years older than I was. Everyone said he was a father figure, but in truth he represented my unconscious desire to find my mother again, someone who could provide the glue and put my life and my family back together. My boyfriend, the disinherited son of an ambassador, was an enormously creative free spirit who drank too much and was often depressed. I didn't have a clue that both alcoholism and chronic depression were serious diseases, and this man did anything but provide the constancy I needed. I was far too young and naïve to understand his complex suffering, and our relationship was rough and stormy from the beginning. Though he was never physically abusive, when he was drunk his verbal abuse was hateful and poisonous. On his good days his bon vivant personality was a perfect backdrop for both the high-flying hippie era and for my personal denial. An unmitigated disaster, my relationship was a perfect mirror of my confusion and numbness. Denial is greedy for company, so I just stuffed my unhappy relationship right next to my grief about Mom's death. The padding around my heart was growing thicker and thicker.

Even though I was closed down on the inside, it's shocking how well I functioned on the outside. Like my actual childhood, my last fling with innocence was full of imagination and adventures. It was the rich creativity that saved me in my hippie years. Just like a kid, I wanted all pleasure and no pain. And pleasure was the *raison d'être* of the Pumpkin House, where we had every kind of drug, every kind of sexual liaison, and constant live rock music. Indeed we paid the highest homage to the trinity of sex, drugs, and rock and roll.

Our commune had its very own rock-and-roll band called Flavored Air, in honor of our preferred drug, nitrous oxide. Flavored Air was an unabashed Grateful Dead rip-off. Devout in our belief that the Grateful Dead was the band for radical poetic hippies, our commune aspired to live by the lyrics of their songs. I was one of the most faithful groupies, following the band to all their gigs and dancing like a wild harpy in long flowing skirts. Playing in bars all over New

England, our band even performed at the Boston Aquarium at the height of its fame. A photo of me as a Flavored Air groupie at the Aquarium is a snapshot of the era. There I am, child-woman in a midnight blue velvet dress hemmed with tiny silver bells, my long hair woven with flowers, eyes outlined with kohl, and a stoned smile on my face.

Renowned for the large hippie parties we threw at a funky old castle on Boston's North Shore, we invited everyone we knew and told them to bring as many people as they wanted. These masquerade balls showcased a gorgeous array of creatures from both land and sea, characters from both past and future eras, and plenty of pre–Harry Potter witches and wizards. As the punch was always spiked with LSD, conversations with these costumed characters tended to evoke a variety of mystical experiences and past-life flashbacks. Alas, I don't think these were the kinds of festivities my mother had in mind when she insisted that every woman has to know how to throw a great party.

Nonetheless, Mom had taught me well and I tried to be the best host possible. At one particular masquerade I dressed as one of my favorite heroines, Catherine the Great. My face powdered chalk white, I wore a high-waisted golden gown and a tall headdress trailing with black satin ribbons. As the great lady, I had had plenty of the LSD punch and was regally serving a large platter of deviled eggs when an iridescent green dragon caught my attention, her long tail suddenly seeming to take over the entire room. I dropped the platter and dozens of slippery deviled eggs went flying and bouncing and splattering across the room. All the while Flavored Air was cranking out Grateful Dead tunes . . . *Truckin', got my chips cashed in. Keep truckin', like the doodah man. Together, more or less in line. Just keep truckin' on.* As the spaced-out queen cleaned up a seemingly endless number of eggs on her hands and knees, no one skipped a beat on the dance floor.

Like our gurus said, just keep on truckin' on. That was the philosophy we lived by.

When we weren't pleasure seeking we took our mandate to change the world seriously. The Pumpkin House commune performed street theater, created a free school for children, ran a bustling food co-op, and had a traveling gypsy restaurant wagon serving tasty vegetarian food, which we drove around to craft fairs. At the center of many of these activities, I had found a perfect outlet for my natural leadership abilities. I was a superb organizer and get-things-done person. Born an entrepreneur, I loved the creative challenges of doing things outside the system. My days were rich and vital, the mornings filled with teaching the children at our school; then dashing over to the food co-op to unload crates of fruits and vegetables, followed by being the cashier at the register; now grabbing a cup of soup and running off to the evening's commune meetings and rehearsals for street theater. The busier I was the less I had to feel. Though I would soon give up all drugs, my addiction to busyness as the most potent way to close off the heart would poison me for decades to come. The split between my inner life and my outer life wedged itself deep into my core. My masculine was on overdrive and my feminine was buried alive.

A wild period doomed to crash and burn, my hippie days came to an inevitable end when my relationship became untenable and my boyfriend and I went our separate ways. Though I remember those Pumpkin House days as a time of enormous creativity when we were all passionate about creating a new and better world, I was also a lost soul. Those strange and heady days of the seventies when our self-centered freedom was everything, while Watergate blew up and Pol Pot reigned and Buddhists monks set themselves on fire, demonstrated that tyranny still ruled the world. I was a perfect reflection of those paradoxical times. On the outside my hippie days were untamed, creative, and free. But on the inside I was not free. I was trapped in denial, caught in the confusion of not knowing who I really was, and stuck in a relationship that could never work. Along with my generation, I was too young to understand that real freedom has its roots in the interior; only then can it sustain itself in the exterior world. Many years later, working with immigrants from all over the world who struggled to make sense of the American concept of freedom, they would often say to me, "Gail, you Americans are free on the outside but it's strange how many of you are not really free on the inside." They are right. Freedom is a complicated matter.

Growing Up and Finding
the Love of My Life

During those untamed years of my twenties I rarely thought of my mother nor did I discuss her death with anyone. My hippie lifestyle of drugs, rock and roll, and saving the world provided the perfect camouflage for my grief.

From the mid-seventies to the mid-eighties I was active in the blossoming human potential movement. Part of an alternative culture in which just about everything was an experiment and outside the bounds of the mainstream, I had found the ideal place for an outsider who loved diversity. It was a perfect place not to fall into my mother's trap of trying to fit in at the expense of one's own dreams.

Along with being part of the first wave of holistic massage therapists in the Boston area, I also made my living as a trainer for the New Games Foundation. New Games was made world famous by the San Francisco counterculture pioneer Stewart Brand. Stewart coined the phrase "Play Hard, Play

Fair, and Nobody Hurt," saying that this was the only necessary rule in New Games. The New Games philosophy em-
phasized cooperation over competition, win/win instead of
win/lose, and inclusion rather than exclusion. Stewart said
that these values were the necessary antidote to Vietnam and
Nixon. He believed that play was a key to the imagination as
well as to harmony among all people. This just about summed
up my life philosophy as a young tomboy on Brecks Lane, so
I felt completely at home.

We offered New Games trainings all over the country,
from small towns in Mississippi and Wyoming to cities like
Seattle, Chicago, and Atlanta. Teaching games like Tweesli
Woop, Ooh Ahh, Catch the Dragon's Tail, Snake in the
Grass, Smaug's Jewels, British Bulldog, and Vampire, we inspired people to keep playing no matter how old they were
or how hard life was. We played with people of all ages and
ethnic backgrounds, and trained every imaginable popula-
tion including people confined to wheelchairs, mental hospitals, nursing homes, prisons, and the amazing people at the
Perkins School for the Blind. At the end of each training
we sponsored a New Games Play Festival, open to the entire
community. Twenty-five years later I can see how visionary
our approach was, offering a creative experiment in diversity
and cooperation.

A particular New Games training in New York City in
1980 would change my life forever. A strikingly handsome
man in bright orange and green running clothes caught my
eye, and later my heart. David Gershon was attending the
training so he could get some ideas for the book he was writing on running. His first impression of me was not that positive. A lifelong vegetarian, he watched me devour three hot
dogs smothered with mustard and relish during the lunch
break. Later we would engage in a heated boffer fight using

the Styrofoam swords popular in New Games. David's sword-play was intense and focused; I just wanted to have fun. And so began my relationship with the great love of my life, the man who would become both my husband and my partner in creating my life's work, the man who would provide the stability I needed to help me grow up and find my true calling.

David and I fell head over heels in love and began our weekend romance, commuting between Boston and New York. Driving my little white Honda Civic with no heat to warm me during the winter months, I arrived teeth chattering at David's West 22nd Street apartment right around the corner from the famed Chelsea Hotel. Soon we would tumble into bed, catching up on our lives and our lovemaking, and then eat large bags of the then-famous David's Chocolate Chip Cookies. My soul mate had lived in New York City for eighteen years, and he knew the city's neighborhoods like the back of his hand. After getting our fix of David's Cookies we would take off, hoofing all over New York while I fell more in love with both the man and his city. For romance there is simply no place like New York; music and theater, candlelight dinners and jazz clubs, the city doesn't sleep and neither did we.

David was a passionate runner, clocking ten miles a day and helping the colorful Fred Lebow organize the first New York City Marathons. After his runs, we would meet in Central Park for walks and wonderful talks. Strolling past the landmarks he cherished from hundreds of hours of running—the Obelisk, Sheep's Meadow, Strawberry Fields, and the Reservoir—I came to know my future husband. He was an unabashed idealist, a visionary who felt we could make the world a better place, and he had committed his life to this end.

"You see, Gail, everyone talks about how bad things are, so what we need is to engage more citizens in improving things. I am working on the strategies for changing people's behavior so they really *want* to take better care of their communities and schools, and the environment. I am all about empowerment," he said, using the word that would later become our claim to fame. "I want to help people fulfill their dreams."

Neither one of us was conscious of the power of that phrase. Walking hand in hand through Central Park, we couldn't have known that the next decades of our life would literally be dedicated to just that, helping people follow their highest aspirations. And David didn't know that his words had tapped into the deepest part of my psyche, a desire to honor my mother by never giving up my own dreams.

In those early days, the truth be told, I thought David's bold ideas sprang from a case of a healthy male ego. But after several decades of watching the man on the front lines of peace keeping, inner-city neighborhoods, education, terrorism, and now the fight against global warming—I can say he's true to his word. He's become one of the foremost experts in large-scale behavior change. And as his colleagues love to say about him, "No one has stranger bedfellows than David Gershon. Who else has worked seamlessly with UNICEF, mayors and senators, the heads of solid waste, water, and energy departments, all snuggled up with police, fire, Homeland Security, and the Department of Justice?" Hans Janitchek, his friend from the United Nations, once called David a graceful revolutionary. I think this is the truest definition of my husband.

Within six months we knew we wanted to get married. I couldn't wait for David to meet Pop, so we took off for the Jersey Shore, where my father had resettled when he married Evelyn. We spent much of the day at his shop, where he repaired and refinished antiques in his retirement years. All those wonderful smells of pine, walnut, and maple flooded back from my childhood as we watched Pop engage in his craft, a master of his trade. This was the place where I most wanted David to know my father.

Before dinner, his whiskey-on-the-rocks in hand, Pop confided in David. "Son, I can't tell you how relieved I am that my daughter is going to spend her life with you. Gail has had her wild times, but I have never been so worried about her as these few last years." He was referring, of course, to my recent relationship fiasco and my dubious hippie lifestyle in the Pumpkin House.

Graciously, David responded that he had been much too serious when we'd met, and that my wild side was good for him. He beamed as I blushed. After another whiskey my relaxed and happy father said, "Let's celebrate your engagement with a night of gambling in Atlantic City." Dressed to the nines, off we went to the casinos, where amid the shuffling cards and rolling dice, my father and I both knew that this time I had been very lucky in love.

Just a month after David and I decided to get married, I had one of my rare but vivid dreams about my mother. The dream was on Easter Sunday morning, a day she especially cherished. As in previous times, she appeared seeming just to visit me. But then, for the first time that I could remember, I dreamed about the actual moment of Mom's death. Her soul left her body like a soft white ribbon disappearing in between the sky and the ocean, slipping through the invisible doorway into the eternal. Though it would still be a long time before I let go of her, it's easy for me to imagine that might have been the moment my mother let go of me.

So it seemed that both my parents had blessed my marriage. Now that we were joining our lives, David and I had to find a place to live. We looked on a map and landed in the Hudson River Valley near Woodstock, New York. The only other time I had been near the little town was for the famous

Woodstock music festival in 1968, when the intrepid Joanie and I got stoned, mesmerized, and muddy as Arlo Guthrie and Joan Baez, The Jefferson Airplane, and Jimi Hendrix made history. With straight faces we had told Mom that we were going to a Bach music festival. Watching the rock festival on television, our mother knew exactly where we were. Thirteen years after that caper, David and I ostensibly chose Woodstock because it was close enough to both New York and Boston that we could travel to either place for work until we had phased out of our current careers and embarked on a new one together. David did the house hunting and found a unique A-frame nestled between the southern Catskills and the Shawangunk Mountains. Our home, which we have lived in for over twenty-five years, has stunning views of the Ashokan Reservoir and our venerable mountain guardians: Ashokan Highpoint, South, Table, Lone, Balsam Cap, Slide, The Wittenburg, Indian Head, and Overlook.

Surrounded by an intimate circle of friends and family, David and I were married in our beloved mountain home on a windy October day. The yellow of autumn blended with my bridesmaids in apricots, burgundies, and purples, and rainbows arched over the house as we exchanged our vows. We acknowledged both David's father, who had recently passed away, and my mother. After the ceremony our guests feasted on the wedding buffet that all our friends had helped prepare, and the giant carrot cake bedecked with swans that pleased David no end. Still wearing the white satin Victorian gown that Joanie had made for her own wedding, I snuck out for a few minutes to play stickball with my nephew Jake. David keeps a photo of this image on his desk, saying that it shows my essence as an elegant woman who is still a tomboy at heart. Though our friend Bob gave us wedding waltz lessons on the rooftop of his New York penthouse, we ended up dancing mostly to reggae that day. As Bob Marley's tunes got us all moving, I felt dozens of the tiny buttons on my dress, from its high collar to its ruffled bottom, begin to pop and spill like wedding confetti. Too happy to be embarrassed, I took it as a sign of my exuberance.

My mother's absence at my wedding left a gaping hole to which I was, at the time, utterly blind. My friends and family were all there to help on the day of my marriage, but there had been no one to assist me in planning the myriad details of invitation lists, the dinner, the cake, the minister, the marriage ceremony, and getting the house ready. No one whose very presence would add special grace to that important day, assuring that everything would go exactly as it should. By then I was so used to taking care of everything myself that I didn't even know there was any other way. On that day when the singularly powerful bond between mother and daughter is especially alive, I didn't even know that I was missing something.

Sun and Moon
Becoming the Empowerment Couple

In October 1981, two weeks after David and I married, on a wing and a prayer and almost no money we launched our company, Empowerment Training Programs. Symbolic of the parallel tracks of our marriage and work partnership were those early weeks that David and I spent hunched over our kitchen table meticulously planning the details of our wedding, and then seamlessly turning to the details of our first empowerment workshop. Over the coming decades our work would support thousands of people in many corners of the globe to live more fulfilling lives. In a very literal sense, our empowerment work helps people clarify their dreams and gives them the tools for manifesting their visions in their personal, professional, and societal lives. Have all these people's dreams made up for Mom's unfulfilled ones? Can being a dream keeper make up for things that are forever lost?

David and I created our work on pure instinct, as if we were answering a call that we had been waiting for all our lives. We both felt we had come together not just as husband and wife but also as fellow visionaries longing to offer our ideas to the world. Neither of us had specific training or back-ground in helping people follow their dreams but we were absolutely following our own dream by creating this work.

"Listen, Gail, this is the early eighties and people are fed up with gurus. Empowerment is the opposite of gurus, it helps people find their own truth in the different areas of their lives. And it respects all kinds of diverse paths. No one way is The Way." David spoke intensely, the way he always spoke when we were working. Having spent many years with a spiritual guru, he knew all too well the underbelly of that beast.

"Yes, I've always loved the image of the cosmic wheel for a nondogmatic approach, many spokes all leading to the same hub of universal truth. Maybe that could be part of our logo." This was such an interesting juncture in the human poten-tial field, when the early innocence and idealism began to mature into more pragmatic and inclusive values that would attract the mainstream. "And David, it's really important to me that empowerment emphasize wellness, not disease. So much healing is about pathology and fixing what is broken. I want our work to be about vision and how to create and manifest dreams." I spoke completely intuitively, without a clue that we were about ten years ahead of the curve in our approach.

In those early days of heady creativity, we ate, drank, and slept empowerment. Our pillow talk might well consist of David saying to me, "I just got an idea, Gailie, don't fall asleep yet. We have to remember to keep our language, and our model, really clean and elegant. I want to bring this work to the mainstream, in business and education and other con-servative sectors."

"Well, you're better at that than I am. I just want to avoid New Age narcissism and navel gazing. It's really important that we convey that real empowerment is a balance of inner work and an outer commitment to society and the world. You know, my love, I think whether people are New Agers or business executives, what people really want and need is community. We have to make sure we give them an experience of that." We might talk like this for hours, until one of us would finally fall asleep. Then we'd start all over again in the morning.

As it turned out there were lots of people who wanted encouragement and the skills for following their dreams. Whether we were working in Boston, Singapore, the Hague, Montreal, or Moscow, empowering people to follow their deepest impulses was, and is, inspiring life work. After more than twenty-five years, and what David refers to as thousands of flight hours, we are fondly known as the empowerment couple. And now, through our Empowerment Institute, we are training other leaders and passing on our legacy.

From the very beginning David and I were a dynamic entrepreneurial team. He had the big sweeping vision and endless supply of fresh, outside-of-the-box ideas. I was the impeccable detail person, an excellent manager of timelines and people. True to the classic social entrepreneur's profile, we had very little money but unlimited will, imagination, and desire to change the world. And David and I both had that unusual and necessary blend of qualities that leads to entrepreneurial success—naïveté, passion, and complete dedication to our vision.

The tricky part of complete dedication is the extremely fine line between dedication and workaholism. Only now, twenty-five years later, can I look back and separate the life-giving aspects of our entrepreneurial zeal from the poisonous parts. On the nourishing end of the spectrum, David and I were on fire with creativity. We designed our trainings on an empty canvas, applying our ideas like bold, bright brush-strokes. Our field of human potential was still young and fresh, when pioneering and experimenting were the coin of the realm. It was an ideal scenario for two visionaries who dislike nothing more than plodding the tried-and-true path.

"Gailee, we need a metaphor that's simple to understand. Something we can build the whole empowerment model on. It has to be profound and simple at the same time." We were hunched at the kitchen table with piles of yellow legal pads at our side. No computers yet, our original trainings were created in illegible longhand.

"What about a nature metaphor?" I said, looking out at our stunning view of the mountains and reservoir. "We could use the metaphor of a garden." I was remembering with great pleasure the large vegetable gardens I tended both in West Africa and during my Pumpkin House days.

Then, as would so often take place in our co-creation, David would take my intuitive image and fill it in with his strategic mind. He suggested using our five core beliefs—self-responsibility, self-esteem, trust in the universe, positive attitude, and flowing with change—to represent the nutrients required for healthy garden soil. Just as the ground of a garden has to be well prepared before we sow the seeds, the ground of our being has to be well cultivated before we can plant our visions and dreams. Most people try to plant their visions before their inner soil has been properly nourished, and then they're frustrated when the things they want so much don't come to fruition. We both understood that people can't make real change in their lives, or their business, or their community until those five fundamental beliefs are being cared for and cultivated. Now we knew that the first phase of our empowerment process would be preparing the environment for growth.

Immediately I saw that once the ground was ready we could guide people to plant the seeds represented by the visions in our seven areas of life: emotions, relationships, sexuality, the body, money, work, and spirituality. Just like sowing the seeds for carrots, cucumbers, and tomatoes in healthy soil. I especially liked this part of the garden metaphor because it demonstrated that an empowered life devotes equal attention to each of these seven vital areas. Work is no more important than relationships, or money more important than the body, or spirituality than sexuality. And so the second phase of empowerment was born.

As the ideas continued to fly back and forth across the table, now we had to figure out how to fit the qualities that sustain empowerment into our garden metaphor. Both David and I realized how important this was because otherwise people think they just plant the seed of their dream and then they're done. They forget to water, weed, harvest, and put the garden down for winter. Like a real gardener, a truly empowered person understands that the growth process is an ongoing daily practice. This idea was critical to David and me because we weren't interested in giving quick fixes, we wanted to offer people a lifelong practice.

Though he had never tended a garden, David was so captivated by the image that he responded as if he had been a gardener all his life. He suggested that our seven sustaining qualities of commitment, discipline, inner guidance, love, support system, humor, and finding your own truth could be like garden tools. Wheelbarrows and watering cans, hoses and hoes, tomatoes stakes and rakes had now made their way into our empowerment model. Elaborating further on the metaphor, I knew that those tools could sustain a garden but if you just stored them in your little garden shed and never actually used them, then the garden died. Above all we had to inspire people to use the sustaining qualities on a regular basis or empowerment would die. The third and final phase of the process was critical.

Finding the elegant model of the three stages of growth, we both knew we had a breakthrough. Finally, exhausted yet exhilarated, off we would go for a walk along the splendid dike beside the Ashokan, the "place of many fishes," so named by the Esopus tribe because of the rapidly flowing clear water.

In hindsight, the most striking aspect about the design of our life's work was how completely intuitive our process was. In fact, the feminine was alive in all her splendor during these creative sessions. Deeply instinctual, profoundly collaborative, and highly original, our process allowed the strong currents of our intuition to move through us and inform us. Much of our teaching today has remained remarkably close to the original work we created at our small kitchen table looking out at our beloved mountains more than two decades ago.

Once we had designed our empowerment training came the daunting task of presenting the work. We drew on the courage and chutzpah of other colleagues who were also pioneers in human potential: Jon Kabat-Zinn, Sharon Salzberg, George Leonard, Ilana Rubenfeld, and Jean Houston. The zeitgeist of both our time and our innovative field was to boldly break new ground. Our audacity can only be described as formidable. Flying by the seat of our pants David and I guided hundreds of people through their life stories, stories full of joy and sorrow and the pathos of the human condition. We had no idea what an enormous privilege this would be, this witnessing of a person's fondest dreams and deepest sorrows. And more than anything that's what we were, witnesses. We listened well, we provided a safe and creative space, and we gave people good tools. And as the years went on and hundreds of people turned into thousands, we became master trainers. Indeed, it was these marvelous people who came to our workshops who trained us. It was their trust in us, their courage to tell their stories with all the glorious and gory details, and their tears and laughter that taught us what we needed to know. Each was utterly unique in his or her particular life story, and at the same time so universal in the longings of the human heart. In the following decade of the nineties, stories would also be at the heart of my own healing journey.

More than anything David and I learned that people from every walk of life, whether they lived in America, Europe, Russia, or Asia, were starved for spiritual community, for a place where they could be with kindred spirits to talk openly about their deepest interior lives. They hungered for a place where differences were celebrated and diversity was understood as the foundation for the future. As the rigid patriarchal dogma of so many traditions—including Christianity, Judaism, Buddhism, and Communism—began to fail people, individuals started to look for alternative places to search for meaning and support. And as the intense speed of outer life threatened to overtake the gentle pace required for genuine inner searching, people sought spaces where they could slow down and quietly review their lives. By luck and instinct we had created work that offered two of the elements most hungered for in modern existence: community and time for interior reflection. Starved for the feminine, the nourishment from these two basic elements was quickly absorbed by people who came to our trainings.

I found tremendous fulfillment in my work. It was pioneering and creative, it helped many people lead more meaningful lives, and as time went on it provided a highly lucrative income for David and me. But like most good things, my abundant success had an ample underbelly. Passion can turn so quickly into workaholism, and collaboration can reverse itself into power struggle. More and more I began to compare myself with David as we taught our workshops. I started to see him as smarter, funnier, and a better teacher than I was. In my eyes people clearly liked him more than me. He was strong and compelling, and I was gentle and inconsequential. I imagined myself a small wilting violet sitting next to a powerful fast-running river. I was falling directly into the pit of my mother's betrayal of her feminine. Now the monsters from my childhood kitchen table, where I took sides with my father's superior rational worldview and ridiculed my mother's emotional intelligence, were coming back to eat me alive.

With pitch-perfect irony we sent people home from our trainings empowered and happy while we went home to vicious power struggles. "David, you did what you always do, you took all the space in the last session. You answered every question and your comments on spirituality and purpose went on twice as long as we had planned. And you are so damned intellectual. Can't you just give me equal time in the workshop? I am so fucking tired of this!" Try as I might to remain cool and calm, I mostly ended up screaming at the top of my lungs.

"For chrissake, Gail, just stand up for yourself. Take your goddamn space, no one is taking it away from you but yourself. Why can't you just grow up for a change? And by the way, your presentations are vague and emotional."

"Oh God, you are so fucking arrogant! You will never get it, will you?" Slamming the door, sobbing, I retreated to our bedroom where I curled myself into the smallest possible shape I could become.

As time went on and David didn't "give me my space," I decided to try to be like my husband, like my father. But no matter how hard I tried to present our model or answer people's questions with David's penetrating laser focus, I couldn't do it. The more I tried to think rather than feel my way into people's queries and dilemmas, the more lost I became. I began to hate myself and to doubt that I had anything to offer. I was dropping further down into the pit of Mom's abandonment. Down, down, I slid into the bottomless pit of our collective abdication of female wisdom.

Still in our early thirties, David and I were much too young to understand that we were playing out the archetypal power struggle of reason over emotion, sharp insight over diffuse awareness—masculine over feminine. But we loved each other and we loved our work, so we kept battling and struggling to find our way. In the end it was, once again, the men and women in our trainings who became my teachers, and my saviors.

At the end of our four-day workshops most people would offer their gratitude, either thanking us before they left or sending long heartfelt letters in the days that followed. Over and over I would read thanks for my tenderness and compassion, my empathy and intuition, but somehow I couldn't absorb the goodness from these words. I was still comparing myself with David, comparing the thanks that I received to the thanks that he received. How could I have missed the contribution I was making when it was acknowledged as beautifully as it was in this letter: "I have never seen anyone listen the way you do. It's as if your heart had ears. This is what I will remember about you, Gail. And you showed me how vulnerability can be a great strength. You have become my role model for a woman leader."

Only now do I see that my refusal to receive the nourishment from these words was imprinted at my birth. I think often of the fact that when I was born I was hopelessly allergic to my mother's milk. Just minutes after my birth, I spat out the essential nourishment of the feminine. Formula and cow's milk were tried to no avail, and finally I accepted goat's milk, to my parents' enormous relief. But the truth is my capacity to receive this female nourishment had been stolen long before my birth. It was stolen away from me by the long patriarchal lineage that demanded that the masculine dominate the feminine, rather than live together as equal partners. How then was I to take back what had been abandoned for so long by me, and my mother, and the world? How then was I to finally take back what I had rejected at birth, what I had refused from my mother, what had been handed down to me by an ancient lineage of wise women?

Indeed it will take me the rest of these pages to answer these questions, but slowly and inexorably I did begin to see who I was. I did begin to claim my birthright as a wise woman. Letters of acknowledgment from the people I worked with continued to pour in from many corners of the globe. They and many others helped me return to my mother's house. I think now that taking back my feminine was a like a holy excavation, a layer-by-gradual-layer digging to reclaim the hidden artifacts of untamed imagination, kinship with the mystery, quiet contemplation, feelings and moods, and the fluid spaciousness that embraces paradox, mending the opposites of life into a whole.

I no longer aspire to be acknowledged for my sharp strategic analysis of a situation, or my ability to have a rational answer for everything. Now when I receive a letter like the following, I can absorb its nourishment and feel deeply seen. "Gail, you seem to understand people with your heart and David understands with his mind. We need both and we need to see them working together as equals. It's a good thing that you and David are so different."

As the conscious feminine knows, we require others to reflect us. We can never really see ourselves unless we're in relationship to others. Because of the nature of my work I was especially blessed to have many people reflect the beauty and power of my female wisdom. It was their hunger for the inner life, space for contemplation and creativity, that began to feed my own essence until many years later it has become strong and fully mature. How I wish my dear mother could have had such angels to hold a mirror to her wisdom. How I wish that I could have been one of those angels.

The more I embraced my own female wisdom, the more I began to feel proud of rather than jealous of David. These days David and I work as true equals, each of us fully in our power. I have learned much from his sharp strategic way of guiding people, penetrating to the very core of their dilemmas. And he has learned from me when to be radically present by listening deeply, shedding a soft light that illuminates the truth in a gentle yet profound way. Just after we were married David and I went on a vision quest with our dear friend Joseph Jastrab. During those inspiring days under Joseph's skilled direction we were asked to choose our vision quest names, names that reflected our deepest nature. David chose Sun Eagle and I chose Laughing Moon. As the years unfolded and we grew into these archetypes, we came to fully appreciate that life requires both the strong light of the sun and the soft light of the moon.

Workaholism
Subversive Enemy of the Interior

Just as I began to have confidence in my own wisdom, there was a subversive force waiting to strangle the very breath out of my nascent feminine. A wise friend once said to me, "If you don't watch out, Gail Straub, your monumental ability to manifest is going to lead to workaholism and burnout." I had a long road to travel before I realized what she was talking about, before I would finally understand that the healthy creative juices of passion could quickly turn sour and toxic if the quiet interior space from which they are born is not honored.

In the early years of my life with David in Woodstock, I gladly, though unconsciously, used the drugs of overwork and speed to numb my grief and barricade the door of my heart. My work was a vehicle for subtle heartfelt transformation, but I was driving it like a bulldozer on overtime. I lovingly led people into the inner sanctum of their feelings, dreams, joys and sorrows. I helped them balance their fast-paced outer lives with their need for quieter, slower, interior time. I reconnected them with their creativity and need for the symbolic realms. Like all the people I guided, I too needed someone to help me with these very things. But I was far too busy to be aware of this, and even more significant, I was sure that I never needed help. To admit that I needed assistance would require me to bring back the presence of the person who had graciously helped me for so many years. It would mean admitting how much I missed my mother's help, admitting that her absence left a gaping hole in me. To receive support I would have to be as brave and open as all the hundreds of people who came to my workshops.

When the maternal influence in a family, a community, or a culture dies, the interior compass is gone and most of our life energy turns outward. When my mother and my family died, I shut the door to the inner world of my feelings and intuition, to stillness and contemplation. I turned completely outward to my work and the world, to activity and accomplishment. The priorities in the dominant culture colluded with the distorted use of my animus: work harder and longer; concrete accomplishment is all that really matters; separate your head and your heart and then it's easy to compartmentalize your feelings.

Fraught with irony, my personal brand of workaholism was in part motivated by my desire to make up for my mother's unfulfilled dreams while it helped others find their true dreams. My work took thousands of people on a rich interior odyssey as my own inner life became more and more barren. Though it takes the slow boat, irony can lead to salvation. For many years, until the coming crisis of my father's death would lead me into therapy with Bert Shaw, my workaholism would remain the most subversive enemy of my authentic feminine. Only with Bert's help would I come to understand that emotional intelligence and depth can never thrive in a climate of speed and overdrive. Only with his help would I understand why I had fallen so completely under the seductive spell of workaholism.

The period of my life that most characterizes the fine line between passion and workaholism, the seductive nature of working too hard, was in the mid-1980s when David and I created the First Earth Run. David had always wanted to mount a global event, and after his experience as director of the Olympic Torch Relay at the 1980 Winter Games, he felt ready. During the Olympics he witnessed the mythic dimension of the torch and its capacity to touch people. Now he wanted to take a torch of peace around the world to inspire global cooperation. After several years of doing our empowerment work with individuals, David was especially curious to see if we could apply our principles to a large-scale social event. The next three years of our lives were utterly consumed with finding out.

We had no funding and knew barely a soul who could help us. It was the audacity of innocence that kept us going. David's mom had died a year earlier, and we used his small inheritance to fund our global initiative in the start-up phase. I have often wondered if this caused Sylvia Gershon to feel proud or to turn over in her grave, most likely some of both. We worked fourteen- to sixteen-hour days for the next few years. Most of our staff volunteered their time and we all flew by the seat of our pants.

One early assignment found me traveling to Singapore, Malaysia, Indonesia, Bangladesh, and India. At each of these stops I was to find people who would volunteer to help us set up the First Earth Run event in their country. Each country's ceremony was to include a high-ranking dignitary—often the head of state—welcoming the torch of peace, followed by regional song and dance celebrating the spirit of cooperation and the awarding of Earth Run medals to the most successful grassroots efforts promoting peace and social justice. I had exactly two weeks to find the right organizers in all five countries.

My guileless demeanor and genuine enthusiasm for the First Earth Run was contagious. Because our vision was simple and compelling (this was the heart of our empowerment model)—a torch of peace representing world cooperation, shedding light on the unsung genius of humanity, and raising money for the neediest kids—remarkable people came forward to orchestrate the event in their respective countries. Irma in Jakarta was a beloved grassroots organizer who told me her life story on the clay rooftop of her simple home; Peter in Singapore was a wealthy dental surgeon who drove me around in his white Mercedes; Ahmed in Dacca was a brilliant young university student who loved his country more than anyone I have ever met; and Kavita in New Delhi told me why she had dedicated her life to serving the poorest children in India as we sat in her elegant rose-scented garden drinking strong chai tea. Each of them would organize stirring events to receive the global torch of peace, ceremonies filled with the dance, music, theater, and pomp and circumstance of their culture. They all volunteered long hours on top of already full lives.

I returned home to New York profoundly inspired by these people. Indeed it was the knowledge of their lives that kept me going throughout the grueling pace of these years. Looking at the large world map with small red pushpins that traced our eighty-six-day route, David and I would then decide where I needed to go next. Soon I was off to Costa Rica, Argentina, and Brazil; Nigeria, the Ivory Coast, and Senegal; Hungary, Poland, and Czechoslovakia; or the endless expanse of China. Since my first trip to Paraguay at seventeen, I had fallen madly and insatiably in love with the diversity of our world. Now I could barely contain my joy.

When I wasn't in some other country I put in fourteen-hour days at our office in the UNICEF headquarters. After work I would head downtown to our pied-à-terre in Chelsea, stopping every night at the famed Empire Diner for my eleven o'clock dinner. I was a familiar site at the Empire, sitting with my reams of telexes (yes, this was long before e-mail or even the fax machine) from Beijing, Moscow, Nairobi, Sydney, or Katmandu spilling off my lap. As I ate my favorite avocado and Swiss cheese on whole wheat, the diner would fill up with actors and musicians who had just finished work and gathered to eat and relax. Some fabulous New York talent would play the funky piano and soon Broadway show tunes melded with messages from Gennadi in Moscow or Zhao in Beijing.

While I was bouncing around the world, David was trying to secure sponsors and partners to fund our initiative. In fact, it wasn't until about six months before the launch that we knew for sure that the First Earth Run would take place. But even before the funding was secure, David had more than thirty heads of state and fifty countries committed to the event and far along in their process of realization. As word got out about the global grassroots effort, more and more countries wanted to join, including both Israel and the Arab States, who had been reticent in the beginning. Were we crazy? Yes, I think probably so. Was there an inordinate amount of grace surrounding this endeavor? Yes, without a doubt.

Eventually, the First Earth Run would become the most significant event for the United Nations' 1986 International Year of Peace, as a global team of runners carried a torch of peace around the world. In special ceremonies in over sixty countries, the torch shed light on a myriad of the kind of courageous grassroots actions that make the world a better place but never reach the attention of our media. Earth Run medals were awarded to various ingenious projects including the collective of women in a tiny African village who irrigated a small plot of land during a famine so that several villages could eat, the volunteer university students in Malaysia who started a national campaign to end illiteracy, and the mother from inner-city Philadelphia who opened her home as a safe place for her son and his friends to kick crack. In the end,

ABC's *Good Morning America* covered the event every week for the duration of the eighty-six-day epic journey, and more than twenty-five million people participated. Partnering with UNICEF, the high-profile nature of the event also raised several million dollars of donations for the neediest children on the planet.

Passion for the vision and our amazing team around the world fueled my workaholism. I was often exhausted, sick from various bouts of dysentery, or overwhelmed by the immensity of our undertaking. But, as any workaholic will tell you, it's the heady mix of exhilaration and exhaustion that becomes addictive. In retrospect, those Earth Run years will remain among the most creative and fulfilling in my life. A partial diet of workaholism can enrich and invigorate but a steady diet can kill us, both emotionally and physically. It's when we don't know when to stop, when we constantly need more and more, when we simply can't say no, and when we are no longer capable of slowing down or enjoying quiet, that workaholism shifts from something creative into something dangerous. Now we don't even realize that we no longer have an interior life, that our feminine has been strangled alive. It was after the First Earth Run that my workaholism became dangerous.

David and I returned home to our life in Woodstock in early 1987. We were broke and utterly burned out. A friend from UNICEF who had lived in Nepal suggested that trekking the Himalayas was a sure cure for serious cases of burnout. Using the last of our savings for our plane tickets, we left home with just our backpacks. Hiking for six weeks through those majestic peaks and hospitable villages of Nepal, we began to heal. It was just David and me and our indomitable sherpa, Porba, and most of our days we walked in silence. Porba took us off the beaten trails and we found our quiet matched the unspeakable beauty of the Himalayas, with its massive snow-covered peaks, sky bluer than any other blue in the world, ancient rickety wooden bridges haphazardly draped over rushing streams, and ridges on fire with magenta and orange rhododendron. In the late afternoon we would stop to make camp, and Porba would serve us steaming hot chai. We would sit surrounded by colorful prayer flags, the sunset turning the sky into lavender, and the immense presence of Annapurna and Machhapuchhare always watching us and minding us.

Nepal took care of our burnout and restored us. Alas, the seductive spell of workaholism in combination with the fact that we were completely broke pushed us into overdrive to get our business going again, and the quiet rhythm of the Himalayas was soon abandoned. Our empowerment work was well known in the Northeast, but now we branched out to Minneapolis, Seattle, Portland, Austin, and Orlando. Soon, with the incredible contacts we had made during the Earth Run, we added Moscow, Singapore, Shanghai, Stockholm, and the Hague. All this took an intense amount of marketing, administration, and travel, not to mention the endless supply of energy required to deliver the trainings. We got a contract to write a book about our empowerment work; we were asked to speak at lots of conferences both at home and abroad, to sit on boards and advise people. I was on a roll. Rolling on the conveyor belt of workaholism, faster and faster, more and more, do more and you will be loved more. Too much, too fast, no pause, no pleasure. All exterior, no interior.

Often it takes a shock to stop this kind of powerful addictive speed. In less than a year I would learn that my father was dying, and then I would finally come to see that I was too. But before I faced Pop's death it was my time to decide if I was going to give birth.

Choosing Not to
Have Children

My own commitment to childlessness remained
virtually unbroken as I grew from child to adolescent to adult to non-parent. But *why?* Why, in the
face of powerful social expectations and pressures,
have I—and millions of other women—elected
to remain "without child"?
                    —Rochelle Ratner, *Bearing Life*

I'm not sure exactly how I decided not to have children.
There are so many interwoven threads making up my choice
that it is impossible to single out one strand, but the inex-
orable imprint from my mother is a more vivid thread than
any of the others. I always felt a subtle yet profound tension
in Mom. Even as a young adolescent I knew that I robbed my
mother of her creative time, that the demands of being our
mother took away something that she longed for perhaps as

much as she loved us. And as I grew older I understood the enormity of the fact that as the eldest Walsh daughter she had already mothered her seven younger siblings, already spent hundreds of hours changing diapers, feeding babies, quieting cries, and endlessly entertaining younger sisters and brothers. Mom's uneasy struggle between what was automatically ex-pected of her and what really called to her is a tension for-ever embedded in my psyche. Poignantly, I take it as one of her greatest gifts to me.

For a time during the 1970s I lived in a women's collec-tive just outside Cambridge, Massachusetts. My women's consciousness-raising group would meet in my attic room, which looked and smelled like an ancient marketplace filled, as it was, with the African masks, statues, and weavings I had just brought back with me from the Peace Corps. When the seminal book *Our Bodies, Our Selves* came out, it inspired end-less dialogue and debate about our role as women. In those intoxicating times we lived on the nourishment of contem-plating the big questions that our grandmothers and mothers rarely had the privilege to ask: what do we really want from life, how can we contribute to the fabric of society, help women less fortunate than we are, nurture our creativity and our dreams? Can we choose to live with another woman, not a man? Do we really want to marry or to have children? My mother's unsung struggle forced me to think very deeply about the children question.

From our very first conversations about marriage and fam-ily David had told me that he didn't want to have children. Immensely blessed to have a clear sense of his mission in life, David knew that he was here to serve the significant issues involved with societal transformation, which he has done with passion and skill throughout the more than twenty-five years of our marriage. He knew that he could not do his work in the world and be the kind of father he would have wanted to be. From the very beginning he also said that if I wanted children we would, of course, have them. But implicit was the understanding that I would be the one doing most of the parenting. I was still unclear about whether I wanted children. Because we were in our early thirties when we married, I knew I had time to decide.

Now it was 1987. We had completed the Earth Run, our business was booming again, I had just celebrated my thirty-eighth birthday, and the clock was ticking away. All our friends thought, well, finally Gail and David must be ready to settle down and have their family. But I wasn't entirely sure I wanted to have children. Profoundly influenced by the global experience we had just completed, my choice about whether to have children or not had become more complicated. The images of poverty and overpopulation we had witnessed in many of the countries where we had just worked were painfully real to me. On the other side of the equation, I felt deeply connected to the global family, hundreds of members of which we had grown to love during the last three years. Didn't I want to have children so they could be a part of this inexplicably diverse and marvelous human family?

Back at home, I took long mountain valley walks searching for clarity. I pondered being pregnant and giving birth, which many of my women friends described as being far and away the most moving experience in life; the primal pull to continue my lineage; the opportunity to love another being unconditionally. On the other side, I considered the positive social and ecological implications of not bringing another child into our fragile, overpopulated planet. I contemplated how rich and fulfilling my life with David already was, and how many ways there are to give birth in this world.

Just below the surface of these rational considerations deeper currents were stirring. I feel certain that the dissolution of my own family after my mother's death played a central role in my decision not to start a family of my own. My unacknowledged yet potent heartbreak at the loss of my family caused my heart to shout: *Why would you ever start a family when it might be torn apart, when you could lose it all so suddenly, so soon in life?* And then there was my mother's ineffable voice reminding me of the difference between mothering as a calling and mothering as a should. It was her heart's struggle, her genuine push-pull about mothering, and all that she lost by her "choice" to have children that spoke to me most hauntingly during my period of discernment. Mom's voice was reminding me that staying true to the feminine requires conscious choice, listening deeply within and choosing from this subtle interior guidance. Having lost her way to exterior pressures, she was warning me to pay attention.

Ultimately I decided that mothering in the traditional sense was not a calling for me. I have little regret over my choice. What is less clear is whether "I" actually made the decision not to have children. Rather it seems I was given just the right mix of life ingredients, a kind of perfect storm, to make a choiceless choice. Was there space in my tender psyche to really consider having children, or was the imprint from my mother's push-pull about her choice so strong that it left little room than to take the other road? If Mom had lived longer, fulfilling more of her dreams, keeping my family intact, and wanting grandchildren, would I have made a different choice? If David had wanted children, would this have altered our decision? If I hadn't been immersed in a rich, creative, socially conscious life surrounded with a close community friends where just as many women have chosen not to have children as those with families, would this have changed things? Who knows?

David and I did know that this was one of our most important life decisions and we wanted to make it consciously. We decided to honor our choice with a small ceremony. In

retrospect this simple action was deeply significant, and something I suggest to anyone who chooses not to have children.
Our ritual represented the baptism of our life aspirations, our
decision to mother and father in nontraditional ways. On
Valentine's Day we made our choice fully conscious.

We placed a blue flag with the symbol of the earth in the
middle of our living room floor. A cobalt blue vase of red
tulips at the center of the earth symbol reminded us to imbue
our ceremony with beauty and tenderness. Around the earth
we placed four bowls honoring each of the elements: earth,
air, fire, and water. We also chose a symbol that would represent mothering and fathering to each of us. I chose a small
statue of Quan Yin, the goddess of Compassion, which I found
in China. David chose a bundle of sage from the high desert
in New Mexico.

We began with a period of silence and simple prayers stat-
ing our intention to make conscious our choice not to have
children. First we sat by the bowl of water and talked about
what we would lose by not having children.

"We'll never have the opportunity to bring a child into
the world that's a unique combination of you and me," said
David.

"We'll never have the chance to express such love, or experience all the ways we could grow and learn by raising children together," I said. Our tears joined the water element.

Next we sat near the bowl of stones and honored what we
would gain by our choice.

"We'll have more time and energy to contribute fully to
the world through our teaching. I want to offer our teaching
to help people live meaningful and empowered lives," I said.

"And I want to give my energy to helping people create
more sustainable lifestyles and livable communities," David
said quietly. His lifelong commitment to sustainability and
social justice were the strongest fibers of his being.

At the fire element David lit his bundle of sage and offered his commitment to spiritual fathering. "I want to guide and mentor those who are called to work with me. I want to try to be a positive role model of a leader who balances my head and heart, and who walks my talk."

And as we sat with the air element, using the archetype of Quan Yin, I offered my commitment to spiritual mothering. "I want to walk the path of compassion," I said. "And I want to be a spiritual mother for those who are called to work with me. I want to help them nourish their spirit."

As we sat with the four elements, it began to snow in our mountain valley. The white hush filled our home and hearts with an unexpected peacefulness. David and I went out for a long walk in the soft quiet of the snow, feeling a sense of peace about the promises we intended to keep. On that snowy Valentine's Day afternoon little did we know what we had put into motion. Though extremely simple, our ceremony had lasting power for us.

Through the years David and I have felt little regret over our choice not to have children, and both of us seem to have fulfilled our commitment to spiritual mothering and fathering with uncanny clarity. David has mentored many in the field of social action and become a leader with a rare ability to balance action and contemplation. I have honored the lineage of Quan Yin by writing two books on compassion. And as the next years of my life unfolded I would become a teacher in the field of spiritual development, fulfilling the role of spiritual mother to many of my students.

These days a surprising number of young women write to me or come to me at conferences where I am speaking and ask how I made my choice not to have children. First, I tell them that any choice means that you will both gain and lose something. No matter which decision you make, make it consciously, because choice is the greatest blessing we have.

By making conscious choices we respect the sacred feminine. I tell them that many voices influence such a decision. Pay attention to your mother's voice, I say, both its positive influence but especially its shadow and unfulfilled dreams. Listen to the earth's voice and its cries of overpopulation and starvation. Carefully hear your partner's voice and whether his or her motivation to have children is a genuine calling or a convoluted set of societal shoulds. And above all listen to your own voice, the voice that articulates your dreams and your deepest longings. Remember there are many ways to mother and father, many ways to create and nourish life.

The Death of My Father
The Rebirth of My Feminine

Just as I was deciding not to give birth I learned that Pop was dying. And though I didn't realize it, both my mother and I were about to be reborn. Bach and Mozart pulled me through the frequent five-hour drives to visit my father in the nursing home he hated. With requiems and cantatas for courage I rehearsed my questions over and over in my mind. What did you love most about Mom? I need you to tell me about your father's suicide. How did you stay so strong when you had so much loss in your life? Did you realize some of your fondest dreams, my dear father?

Some of the same haunting questions that I had never been able to discuss with Mom before she died so young, I now had to ask my father or I would never have another chance. Those questions about love and pain and dreams, which seemed so easy when presented to people in the workshops I led all over the world, became impossible for me when I arrived in my father's sterile white cubical room. My desperate longing was dwarfed by the ever-present stoicism surrounding my father and his tragic story.

Instead of venturing into unexplored emotional terrain, the territory that would be opened up by the queries burning in my heart, Pop and I spoke of the state of the world and how to live simply in a culture overrun by greedy consumerism. Even after his second heart attack, he still had the energy to rant about the evils of television and the sad demise of honest politicians. I was thirty-eight, my father was eighty-one, and for as long as I could remember it had been this way between us; the universal over the personal, the intellect over emotion, the masculine over the feminine. Always. When my father died I was gifted with his courage and integrity, and imbued with his vital social conscience. I knew that he loved me, but I understood little of how he felt inside. A man of his generation, he trusted that his actions sufficiently reflected his heart.

I never asked those questions that I had repeatedly rehearsed, never got the answers that I so desperately needed, so when Pop died I felt like both a failure and a fraud. Keeping my dark feelings hidden, I pushed my secret failure far away under layers of strong will and worldly accomplishments. My overachieving, more-is-better modus operandi had always worked for me before and surely it would triumph yet again. Secretly I held the belief that since my workaholism was making a moral contribution to the world I should never have to suffer its consequences. But neither my narcissism nor the strength of my considerable will could override this looming depression.

Mercifully my psyche, the crown of the divine feminine, knew the truth. During the day I could fake my way, disguising my secret feelings of sadness and emptiness. But in the dark of night, when the unconscious is ruling queen, my strong rational will didn't have a chance. I began having a recurring dream where I was a bust sharply chopped off just above the heart. I floated through my dreamscape, a disembodied bust with thoughts and ideas pouring out of my head but with absolutely no capacity to feel. All head and shoulders heavy with responsibility: what had happened to my heart and my body? Why was I, a seemingly highly successful woman, feeling so dead? How had I become my father?

Shrouded in denial, I couldn't understand the uncanny precision of the chopped-off bust as a symbol for my life; a life of overdrive, a life of always doing nothing but the best on the outside and never feeling on the inside. That's what I learned from my father, whom I wanted to emulate. Far more painful and insidious, being the best overachieving, unfeeling bust meant that I could make up for my mother's early death by living double time for both of us. I could live not only my own life, but her unlived dreams as well. I began to realize that my heartless bust represented the cut-off partnership of the distorted masculine and the betrayed feminine, my father and my mother. Becoming increasingly exhausted from the lethal combination of outer workaholism and inner denial, finally I called a good friend and told her I was in trouble and needed a good therapist. "Of course, of course, your father just died," she immediately said. It hadn't occurred to me that my depression was related to my father's death, only to my lifelong obsession with achievement. What could that possibly have to do with my father? "Go see Bert Shaw," my friend said. And then, the words that I will never forget: "He's a force to be reckoned with."

On the way to my first visit with the force to be reckoned with I was too naïve to be nervous. As I drove alongside the Beaverkill River, with its quaint bridges crossing over rushing currents, I determined that in just a few sessions I'd be myself again. I arrived at the spacious white farmhouse surrounded by stonewalls, small intimate gardens, and brick pathways, and felt like I was in Ireland, the land of my mother's heritage. I couldn't have known, though, that it would be in this house that I would finally find Mom again.

"Welcome, Gail. Come in and make yourself comfortable," said the handsome white-haired man in a soft blue sweater and jeans. It was a casual disguise for the shaman of my liberation. "How do you feel today, Gail?" I stared into the kind eyes of this wise steady man and decided to trust him. The floodgates of my psyche creaked open.

"I feel like a bust chopped off right above the heart," I said and began to cry. Pop's death had brought me to the doorstep of the man who would become my spiritual father.

"Tell me about your life, Gail. Just take your time, and tell me what's troubling you," said Bert tenderly. In that moment it seemed as if I had been waiting many long years for someone to say these words to me, for someone to help me uncover and face the pain and denial that were just below the surface of my successful life. Someone to listen to my story, creating the alchemy that transforms hurt into healing. Just months after my father's death and sixteen long years after Mom died, my healing journey with Bert would be a turning point in my life. As with so many seekers before me, I would come alive again only when I truthfully faced the death of my parents and all the unresolved questions their passing demanded that I answer.

Over the next several years Bert would help me understand why I felt like a bust chopped off above the heart. All that I had hidden in my heart, all that I couldn't say to Pop as he died, I could finally tell my spiritual father. My desperation to get my stoic father's love had distorted the positive aspects of my masculine energy—will, manifestation, and responsibility— and turned them into overdrive and overachievement. I could see how I had pledged my allegiance to the masculine—reason over emotion, doing over being, the universal over the personal—in order to please my father and the dominant culture that he was inextricably linked to. Understanding all that Pop's death symbolized while simultaneously finding my spiritual father prepared the way for the death of my unconscious masculine and the birth of a conscious animus. In my work with Bert one of my most significant realizations was that I needed a strong healed masculine to help me rebuild my betrayed feminine. In the decade ahead I would slowly learn to use my reason and will in service to my heart and intuition. I would gradually build an equal partnership between doing and being, inner and outer, personal and universal. And once again I believe my personal story is a direct reflection of the larger universal story. Neither men nor women can become whole people until we have healed and balanced both the masculine and feminine aspects within us.

As I understood my father more fully and cultivated a conscious relationship with my own masculine, I was ready to begin the journey back to my mother. I had always considered myself to be my father's daughter but now, much to my amazement, I discovered that at a much more complex level I was equally my mother's daughter. At birth I had rejected my mother's milk, by the time I was seventeen I had left her house, and for sixteen years now I had buried my sizable grief about her death. They say there is nothing more fierce and lasting than the bond between a mother and daughter. Mom had never left me, not for a moment. I began to see how I was living double time, fulfilling both my own dreams and what I perceived to be my mother's unfulfilled aspirations. I took my overcompensation even further as I helped others with their dreams. Unconsciously, I wanted to live for both of us, creating my lifestyle and community in Woodstock as the kind of life I believe Mom wanted and never had. I lived fast and furiously to make up for the life she had lost, as well as to make the most of my time because I feared that I, too, might die at fifty-five. The shadow of my mother's death and unfulfilled dreams cast itself over my entire life.

My workaholism had another more painful part. Far more insidious than my desire to please my father, my overachievement was a futile attempt to get my mother's acknowledgment. Starting my own business, doing trainings all over the world, and writing books was never enough. Mom would never be there to confirm my life, to say to me, "My sweet daughter, you have done so well, you have done enough." The overdrive of the masculine could never replace my need for the absent feminine. And now I could clearly see how precisely I had followed in the footsteps of my mother's betrayal of her feminine. I could clearly see that the epidemic of the father's overdrive in modern culture can never take the place of our longing for the mother's gentle nourishment. I saw that my father's death was the gateway for the rebirth of my feminine, for taking back what Mom and I and so many others had left behind. I knew there was no better way to honor both my parents' lives than to try to reverse this betrayal. My global journey to take back the wisdom of the feminine was about to begin.

PART THREE

Returning to My Mother's House

Taking Back My Wisdom

I was passionate,
filled with longing,
I searched
far and wide.

But the day
that the Truthful One
found me,
I was at home.

—Lal Ded

Healing Time

Finding My Open Emptiness

> The defining of a self is not the same as the defining of a role. I felt fully female, completely identified with my sex. And I felt capacious, roomy, open, and ready to be who I was and take on the tasks that would fall to me. That capacity came from a feeling of *ready emptiness*.
>
> —Molly Peacock, *Paradise, Piece by Piece*

In her stirring memoir about her choice not to have children, the poet Molly Peacock says, "A woman who does not have children, whether she chooses not to have them or simply ends up not having them, is always defined by a kind of minus. Whether she calls herself child*less* or child*free*, motherhood is so entrenched in the definition of female that not mothering comes to be seen as not fully female. The move a woman has to make is from feeling negatively empty to openly empty." Now I feel the open emptiness that Molly Peacock speaks about, but it wasn't always this way. I could only experience it once I was finally willing to grieve my mother.

And my grieving came slowly. My father's death and my healing work with Bert had started my process. The real turning
point came when I had major surgery to remove my left ovary,
which had been taken over by a grapefruit-sized cyst. In certain traditions both the left side and the location of my cyst
in second chakra, the center of creativity, represent the feminine. So literal was my masculine overdrive that it had over-
taken my female center. There was no emptiness in my womb.
It was full of pain and denial, full of overachievement, full of
my mother's death.

Even before the physical surgery, another kind of surgery
took place in my emotional body. Once my operation was
scheduled I had a month before I went into the hospital. During those weeks my strong warrior façade dissolved before my
eyes. Terror visited me in all the forms I had pushed aside for
so long: dread of dying, deep mistrust of my body, and panic
at losing control. I felt I could control my mind, the rational
masculine, but I had little control over my body, the irrational
feminine. I was sure I would die during my surgery. I was a
wreck. A recurring dream underscored my terror.

> I lie dying in a great pool of blood. I watch the blood
> continue to seep out of my body all around me. A man I
> don't know comes to administer CPR. At first it doesn't
> work and the man is about to give up. Then suddenly I
> jump back alive. I awake trembling like a leaf.

This emotional "falling apart" was the first phase in my soft-
ening, in creating an open emptiness for an interior life. Many
years later, I would come to understand that the terror I was
experiencing around my body had started at birth when I refused my mother's milk and came close to dying. The further
connection between an untrustworthy body and death was

imprinted through Mom's long mysterious illness, whose influence was profoundly imbedded in my psyche. Now, as I was coming close to grieving my mother, my terror returned me to the original birth wound that bound us together. Shamans say that our deepest wound is the doorway to our healing. For me this was true, as facing the dread of my body and dying would bring me through the gateway into my grieving.

A few days before I left for Portland, Maine, where my friend and colleague Dr. Christiane Northrup would perform my surgery, I had another dream. Unlike my earlier dream of terror, this dream was comforting and empowering, signaling my readiness to embrace the spiritual lessons of my surgery.

Lying in my hospital bed just after surgery, I hear the voice of my distorted masculine shouting the phrases that have haunted me for so long. "Do more. Accomplish more. Faster! You'll never, never be enough." But then, I see my soft feminine self is standing at the side of my bed stroking my head. She holds the cyst in her left hand and tells the masculine, "Gail's done with this now, she doesn't need it anymore, take it back." And the masculine bows to the feminine.

Chris and I had long talks about my life, and she knew that the surgery was full of spiritual significance for me. She had promised to actually show me the cyst after she had removed it. True to her word, once I had woken up from my operation she brought me my ovary in a small jar. It looked like an angry, overstressed red muscle; all of my overdrive and overaccomplishment seemed contained in that ugly red mass. I realized in that moment that I had sacrificed my ovary to empty my womb of denial, to let go of my need to compulsively fill my emptiness with accomplishments my mother would never see. And yes, I gave up my ovary so I could take back my feminine.

My surgery had another extraordinary irony. Chris knew that I had chosen not to have children, so she asked me if I would like her to do a tubal ligation while she performed my surgery. Yes, of course, this was the perfect moment to free myself from uncomfortable diaphragms and concerns about getting pregnant. So she tied my tubes, and I felt like a free woman. But my dear mother had had a tubal ligation done by her doctor without her consent at the time of Joanie's birth in 1950. The reasoning was that this could save my mother's life; both Joanie and I had been cesarean births and her doctor felt Mom couldn't go through another cesarean because of her fragile heart. But my mother was a devout Catholic, and the tubal ligation caused her excommunication from the Church. Mom was deeply depressed after Joanie's birth. She spent many years with the help of her local priest petitioning the Catholic Church until, finally, late in her life she was accepted back into the fold.

I only learned this heartbreaking information after my father had died, and shortly before my surgery. Jimmy and I were visiting our parents' gravesites, and both Mom and Pop were very present to us. Driving back to his house in Wilmington my brother said to me, "I remember so vividly how Mom was often crying right after Joanie was born. For a long time I thought it was probably postpartum depression or something like that. But after our mother died I asked Pop about it and he told me this amazing story about her tubal ligation and the excommunication that followed." I listened astonished as my brother filled in the details of her years of petitioning the Church and being accepted back.

"That's unbelievable! You mean Mom took us to mass every single Sunday despite this incredible injustice? She even had

Pop convert to Catholicism, and this is what her religion does to her?!" I was stunned into momentary speechlessness.

"I think Mom drew a deep strength from her faith," my brother finally said quietly.

Driving from Wilmington back home to Woodstock, once again I had the feeling I was discovering my mother for the first time. I found her faith astounding and bewildering. Finally I understood why my memory of Mom at mass had always been so wistful and far away. Somehow the full complexity of my mother's life, faith and injustice, joy and suffering, ful-fillment and disappointment, was utterly transparent as she sat at mass. Now I could see that one of her richest gifts to me was her example of how true faith is so much greater than dogma. That, in fact, the essence of the sacred feminine is a faith beyond dogma, a largesse of spirit that can accept par-adox and embrace the unknown. Thinking about all this, I had never loved my mother more.

The timing of my visit to Mom's grave and hearing the circumstances of her excommunication just months before my surgery was grace at work. Understanding my mother's fullness gave me the strength to find my open emptiness. In the terrible irony of our tubal ligations, my freedom and my mother's tyranny, the opposites between us never seemed more poignant. Never had I so appreciated the immense chasm between Mom's devotion to an unjust patriarchal God and my reverence for a nondogmatic Goddess. Never had I felt so strongly how these inexplicable opposites bound us inextri-cably together as mother and daughter. Finally, the tension of these opposites broke open my heart and allowed me to grieve Mom. Our fallopian tubes, the primal essence of our female condition, finally brought us back together. Now I could re-turn to my mother's house.

During the luxurious weeks of healing after my surgery, I

lay propped up in my bed, vulnerable, open, and empty. The physical and emotional trauma of surgery softened me and I was ripe to grieve. I pored over photographs of my mother as a girl, a young woman, a wife, and a mother. I reread the many letters people had written to my father just after Mom died and I saw how greatly she was loved for her kindness and zest for life. I read my final correspondence, the daily get-well postcards in my inimitable twenty-year-old voice, written to my mother from West Africa just weeks after her open-heart surgery. And I read her response written just two days before she died, which carries still my mother's heart-breakingly tender voice.

Dear Mom,

I hope you are feeling better every day. Your last letter said you were coming along slowly but surely. It's raining cats and dogs here! All the new Volunteers have arrived and they are so excited and curious about everything. I am taking some of them to my favorite market place tomorrow. Last week was a holiday and the parades were wonderful. The African women in their hand embroidered robes and high head dresses in indigo, purples, reds, oranges, and yellows. They are just the most beautiful women in the world. There were masks of all kinds and huge puppets on stilts portraying the village stories. The men playing big gourded balafons and drums of every size. And of course everyone dancing, dancing, dancing all through the night. I continue to be challenged by my teacher training and I just hope I will be a good teacher for my African students. Let me know how you are doing Mom.

Love to all, Gail

Dearest Gail,

Sweetie, I just wanted to let you know that I am home
again from the hospital and I am fine this time . . . We
love getting your daily cards and are so happy to hear
that things are going well for you dear, even though a
little hectic. I am sure that you will find teaching a little difficult at first but it will loosen up for you soon dear
one. Everything has a way of opening up for you, am I
right? Don't be discouraged! You always find the way
sweetie.

All my love dear, Mom

During those healing weeks of grieving, twenty years after
my mother's death, I felt the heavy blocked dam finally re-
lease inside me. I was both overwhelmed by the power of my
grief and comforted by the feeling of relief it gave me. I turned
to my favorite women poets—Mary Oliver, Anna Akhmatova, Grace Paley, and Maya Angelou—searching for clues to
help me understand the eternal themes in mother-daughter
relationships. Peering into the prism of these poets' hearts, I
was beseeching them to make sense of my loss, my denial, and
at long last my buried pain. I was beseeching them to tell me
I had not failed as a daughter. Again and again I returned to
Marge Piercy's poem "Crescent Moon Like a Canoe" and these
verses in particular:

In my childhood bed we float, your sweet
husky voice singing about the crescent
moon, with two horns sharp and bright we would
climb into like a boat and row away
and see, you sang, where the pretty moon goes.

In the land where the moon hides, mothers
and daughters hold each other tenderly.
There is no male law at five o'clock.
Our sameness and our differences do not clash
metal on metal but we celebrate and learn.

My muse, your voice on the phone wavers with tears.
The life you gave me burns its acetylene
of buried anger, unused talents, rotted wishes,
the compost of discontent, flaring into words
strong for other women under your waning moon.

My grieving continued and gradually, with Bert's help, I
uncovered and healed more layers. I read Hope Edelman's
groundbreaking book *Motherless Daughters* and wept for most
of three hundred pages. I discovered that my long period of
denial was not unusual for women who lose their mothers at
an early age, and that I perfectly embodied the motherless
daughter profile—strong and self-directed, independent and
self-reliant, and constantly trying to fill the empty space left
by a mother's death.

Even now that I am almost sixty and have accomplished a
great deal in life, I can easily be seduced back into that negative
empty space. Small unexpected glances, conferences full of successful people, a woman friend talking about her mother—any
of these can send me toppling back into that emptiness and
feeling like I can never accomplish enough to fill the void. I
am still learning to navigate the difference between the seductive emptiness that I compulsively need to fill, and the open
emptiness that leaves me free to simply participate fully in my
own life.

Coming Home

Landscape as the
Tabernacle of Memory

How then do we "come home" spiritually and
dwell there? In my own life I have found no better way than to value and savor the sacredness of
daily living . . . Increasingly, it is for me a matter
of being willing "to be in place," to enter into
deeper communion *with* the objects and actions
of a day and to allow them to commune *with* me.
— Gunilla Norris, *Being Home*

As I was healing from my surgery and grieving Mom, important seeds were planted in the new garden of my feminine. I
began to fully inhabit my home, my landscape, and my community. Seeded during the time of my grief, these three elements would become the trinity that empowered my return
to the conscious feminine. Embodying the very things that
uprooted my mother when she left Colorado for the East Coast

would now allow me to firmly plant my life. In the years to come my home would become a sanctuary for my interior life; the surrounding reservoir and mountains a blessed oasis in my full life; my community the family who could hold me. Up until now I had a lovely house but not an embodied home.

My mother was eminently present in our home, as she had taught me well how to create beauty as an abode for the soul. As my parents filled my childhood home with my father's handmade treasures, so we filled our house with furniture of a rich cherrywood, handcrafted by our friend Steve and beautifully showcased by the wooden beams in the A-frame. Here, perched above the Ashokan Reservoir, David and I created a refuge of beauty and simplicity, a place where our imaginations could run free. Situated above the rest of the house, we built a tiny meditation room with stunning views of our mountain valley. This space represented our commitment to a more balanced life of both inner contemplation and outer engagement. Incorporating the ample blue stone on our property, we designed small Japanese gardens as corners of stillness. Wanting to share my true home with friends, this led naturally to the desire for community. With several friends I started the process of gathering a group of kindred spirits to form conscious community. Fifteen years later, we still gather regularly for meditation and prayer; we have sat with loved ones as they passed away; we have engaged in social action and held some of the most exuberant celebrations in the Hudson Valley. We have witnessed one another's joys and sorrows, and if we are truly blessed we will be surrounded by one another at death.

Falling in love with my place and its people, I wanted to be home more and work less. One of the most precious and undervalued gifts of the feminine, this creation of true home was fundamental in breaking the powerful bonds of my workaholism. Home becomes a haven for the interior life only when we truly inhabit the space, spending enough time being, dreaming, feeling, creating, and sharing this with friends. Such a simple thing, this ancient honoring can save our lives.

I knew my mother's central role in teaching me how to create a home, but what was startling was the recognition of how my landscape had mimicked a place where Mom had embodied her authentic creative self. As I settled into my home, I came to realize that the setting of my house in the Hudson River Valley offered a striking reminder of the setting in Maine where my family spent many summers. As a young girl looking out from the small rustic cabin onto Kimball Pond and the White Mountains, with Mount Kearsarge prominent in the foreground, I always felt I was being held by something large and eternal. Now, as an adult, I feel a similar comfort when I look out my window at the Ashokan framed by our Catskill Mountain guardians, and sometimes I am transported back to the Maine landscape that contains the happiest of all my childhood memories.

Along with some of his army buddies, Pop had helped build Camp Ettowah for Boys. The camp was the brainchild of the eccentric Britt Holmes, who had bankrolled the entire endeavor. In the early phases they constructed the dirt road into the Maine woods, a long scented corridor of birch, pine, maple, and endless blueberry hedges in full blossom in the summer months. Over the years my father and his cronies had built the living cabins and activity rooms, the mess hall, and athletic fields that eventually became Camp Ettowah. Just like the army, Camp Ettowah had a bugle player who announced the different periods of the day: reveille, mess hall, retreat, and finally taps at night. Pop was the head counselor at Ettowah, organizing the activities of the day for all the campers. This job might as well have been sent from heaven for my talented father. You could find him in the shop helping an older camper construct a sailfish, or leading a two-week canoe trip down the Saco River, or cheering us all to the summit of Mount Washington. So happy was my father during these glorious Maine summers that it was as if grace poured down on him, making up for all his loss.

A superb athlete, my brother Jimmy reveled in every sports activity he engaged in. Joanie and I were free to create our own rascal tomboy days exploring the creeks and sandy shores, studying loons and bullfrogs and whatever else we might find. Or we might venture into the balsam pine forests collecting the scented needles for the fragrant balsam pillows that Mom had taught us how to make. Every Saturday afternoon the two of us were put to work shucking huge baskets of corn for the entire camp. Our reward for hours of labor was a double-dip coffee ice cream cone, dished out by the rotund camp cook, Mrs. Drew. We were convinced that we had the better end of the deal. Mrs. Drew also held the famous Ettowah Lobster Races on the large slippery wooden floor of the camp kitchen. The poor Maine lobsters would be lined up like a horse race. Then, the adults would place bets on which creature would be first to reach the finish line of the giant pot of boiling water. It took many years before I could enjoy Maine lobster. Joanie and I loved that we lived in a small cottage called the Skunk Cabin, and that Kimball Pond became our second home, hosting us in endless hours of swimming, canoeing, and sailing. I was utterly in my element, as was my sister, the future ecologist. Like an unforgettable first love affair, this Maine landscape haunted me until I found my lasting true love in the Hudson Valley.

All of this is simply fond memories of idyllic summers, but here's the significant revelation. Looking back, I see now that of everyone in my family, it was my mother for whom the days in Maine were most important. No house to run, no meals to cook, no nine-to-five job, and three children happily occupied all day long. Consisting of two small bedrooms, a tiny bathroom, and a screened-in porch, the Skunk Cabin required a daily ten-minute sweeping, and that was it, period. With this blessed time and space, Mom took classes in oil painting and did lovely watercolors of the abundant covered bridges and old general stores in the area. She painted the giant totem pole in front of the camp dining-hall in bright yellow, red, and green native patterns. Lying on the dock reading, she was serene in her strapless blue bathing suit. You could almost hear her murmur, "Simplicity, what a gift sent from the gods." In the cool Maine evenings, she and Pop would join the other camp counselors in the spacious mess hall where we ate all our meals. Chatting or playing cards with their close circle of friends, they sat in front of the big stone fireplace, over which hung a moose head with a Marlboro stuck in his fat lips.

In our Maine photos my mother is vibrant, laughing, and at home with herself. Here she is dressed with her unique flair, a stylish navy linen blouse with large pearl white buttons, a wide red leather belt, and white peddle pushers hugging her hips. Fully embodied, interior nourished, spirit intact, and imagination on fire, Mom has found herself again.

But these lovely summer months must have been both an obvious blessing and also a cruel contrast to the life my mother would not be able to keep for long. As the three of us grew up, camp was no longer interesting to us, and both of my parents needed to make more money during the summer months in anticipation of our college expenses.

My friend the late John O'Donohue, the Irish poet and scholar, spoke of landscape as the tabernacle of memory. There are certain places, he said, that guard the hidden nostalgia, the joys and suffering of shared life. Held in that Maine landscape of mountains and lakes is the happiness of my family and the reality of my mother as a free spirit with a paintbrush in her hand. For more than twenty-five years I have lived in my own spacious landscape of mountains and water. It is in this landscape that I belong, this landscape where my mother's dreams and mine are both alive.

Bali

Searching for the Wisdom
of the Deep Feminine

Surely whoever speaks to me in the right voice,
    him or her I shall follow,
as the water follows the moon, silently,
    with fluid steps anywhere around the globe.
        —Walt Whitman, "Vocalism"

As I came home and was able to grieve my mother, her presence flooded back into me, full of her loving encouragement but also the unresolved themes and questions from her life. I saw so clearly how her betrayal of her emotional intelligence, her artist's intuition and imagination, and the values of her interior life precisely mirrored the universal loss of the feminine in our society. Returning to my mother's house I came upon a great longing to return to my own feminine wisdom, to understand more fully my own allegiance to doing over being, head over heart and body, exterior values over interior attributes. Now I was especially fascinated to explore how my personal journey was a reflection of the universal desire of women all over the world to take back the feminine.

Throughout the decade of the nineties I continued my empowerment work with David but I also began to work with women again, as I had done in the seventies. This time I worked with women in and from vastly different cultures. During this decade the cultures of four distinctly different countries—Bali, Russia, China, and Ireland—would teach me about the many faces of the divine feminine, helping me reclaim my own wisdom and understand my mother more fully.

In 1986, I discovered the magic of Bali during my work in Indonesia preparing for the First Earth Run. In 1991 I offered a trip for women to that isle of enchantment. I was pretty literal in my search for the feminine, and I called the trip "Bali: A Journey into the Deep Feminine." The first paragraphs of my bright magenta brochure read like this:

> On my first trip to Bali a special doorway to my deep feminine was opened. My senses became more awakened than ever before. I felt soft, open, and receptive. I lived from my heart not my head. My intuition was wild with vivid imagination. My dream state was highly animated and deep with symbolism. I was able to slow down, flow, and truly experience being. Quite simply, I was in a state of joy. On one of my later trips to Bali I had a dream in which I journeyed to Bali with a group of women. We visited temples, learned Balinese dance, swam in the sea, made rituals, and lived joyously in the realm of the deep feminine. I invite you to join me in Bali and be part of this dream come true.

The brochure went on to describe the itinerary, which would start with a journey to the mighty volcano Gunung

Agung, the navel of the world and Bali's mother mountain. We would attend a sacred ceremony at the majestic mother temple Pura Besakih, comprised of thirty separate temples in seven terraces built up the side of Gunung Agung. And at dawn on our final day we would climb into the massive outer crater of Mount Batur, Bali's father mountain.

The trip's cost, $3,550 in 1991, was steep to say the least. I received an overwhelming response to the brochure. More than fifty women wanted to go, and some were willing to spend their life savings to reclaim their feminine wisdom. I could take only twenty. Seventeen years later I continue to get e-mails and letters from women who have the rumpled faded magenta brochure and want to know if I am still leading those deep feminine trips to Bali.

Reclaiming the feminine had struck a resounding chord in the hearts of the American, Canadian, and European women who traveled with me on the five trips to Bali over the next several years. In age we spanned the decades from twenty to seventy; we were single and with partners. One woman had nine grandchildren, and another had five daughters. There was a lesbian couple who had adopted a daughter from Vietnam, several of us who had chosen not to have children, and some who were still trying to figure out if they wanted a partner or children. We were a dynamic and diverse group including painters, opera singers, and writers along with corporate lawyers and vice presidents. There were AIDS activists, a doctor running a women's clinic in the inner city, and a woman who had started a shelter for battered women.

What became poignantly clear during these trips was that many women felt their feminine had been stolen away. Stolen away by rape, abuse, or incest. Stolen away by workaholism, lack of role models, allegiance to the idealized father, or a mother who betrayed her own essence. Stolen away by pressure to climb the corporate ladder like a man and pressure to place logic over emotion, product over process. Nurtured by the splendor of Bali's landscape—rice paddies tripping down hillsides like giant steps, volcanoes soaring up through clouds, dense tropical jungles, clear mountain lakes, and most of all the healing waters of the Indian Ocean—we began to take back what had been stolen away from us.

All of us knew we spent too much time in our minds, and we came back into our bodies through daily romping in the sea, walking through rice fields, and lessons in Balinese dance. Our senses were reawakened by Bali's sensuous landscape; the constant visual feast of temple festivals and rituals, the haunting sounds of gamelan orchestras, and the pervasive scent of the temples' clove incense. As the days passed we started to slow down and experience what the Balinese called *jam karet*, or rubber time, indicating an expandable present. Now we could find the quiet open emptiness inside us. In the spaciousness of *jam karet* we could honor our emotions, the deep dark waters of the feminine where our anger, betrayal, denial, sadness, and loss resided.

We sat in a circle on the soft sand under the trees, always near the comforting sound of waves, always the intoxicating scent of frangipani thick in the air. We told our stories and dedicated our time in Bali to reclaiming some aspect of our female wisdom. I told the women in the circle, "This trip is for my mother and her unlived dreams. It's to honor the feminine she both embodied and abandoned. She died nearly twenty years ago, but I have only just recently reconnected with her. She is my silent companion on this trip. I so wish she could really be here with me." The women listened quietly.

Floating on our backs in the warm salty Indian Ocean, which we had fondly dubbed the Great Mother's Womb, we talked for hours about the questions floating in our hearts. Do we want it all—partnership, family, and successful careers? Does having it all in our fast-paced Western world mean that we risk losing our feminine, with her slower, more in-stinctual ancient rhythms? Many of our mothers and grand-mothers had abandoned their true professional dreams to stay home and raise us, or work in jobs just to bring an income, or both. Now that we had the choice of family and careers that we really wanted, we felt that we had to take both or we might betray the progress that women had made. The more we drifted in the aqua sea, the more we realized that every choice had both joy and sorrow. Buoyed by the Great Mother I saw clearly that neither Mom nor I "had it all." But what I had in my generation, and she didn't have in hers, was gen-uine choice. Is this choice then the greatest gift of the God-dess? Thousands of our sisters, in too many parts of the globe, would remind us that this is indeed the highest blessing of all. They would implore us to take this gift of choice and use it wisely and responsibly, both as tribute to our own mothers and as a sign of hope to them.

Overlooking river gorges and palm forests, our bamboo Balinese houses were called Cahaya de Wata, meeting place of the gods. In the cool evenings the jubilant sounds of the village gamelan orchestras would drift across the gorge tempt-ing us into wild dancing, spinning like dervishes across the wide porch floor. Cocooned in mosquito nets and entranced by the tropical night sounds, we slept naked and let our dreams run wild. Each morning we held a dream circle, honoring the potent realm of the unconscious, that place where the irra-tional ruled like a regal queen. One morning I shared a pow-erful dream with the women in my circle:

> I come to a round black and white door designed like the yin and yang symbol. The door opens at the curved line that separates the yin and the yang. Through this door I am following my female lineage where I can see the faces of my mother and grandmothers, and women

ancestors going way back. We enter a stone chamber where there is a large yin and yang symbol on the floor. The yang half is very dominant and the yin takes a much smaller space. My grandmothers are trying to bring the pattern back into proper balance. Suddenly the dream switches to me as a young girl with Mom. Mom is hand-ing me boxes filled with the gifts of her feminine, then she starts to dissolve. But before she disappears I can just hear her say to me, "Help us balance the pattern."

I awoke from the dream weeping. Though Mom had abandoned her authentic self later in life, we had enough years up to my early adolescence where I had fully imbibed her essence. It was inside me; all I had to do was remember it and take it back. And in this dream, in Bali where her true self would have felt so at home, my mother was inviting me to take back what she had lost. Not just for myself and for her, she was telling me to do this for so many of our sisters around the world.

The time I most ached for my mother during these trips was in the experience of Bali's exuberant artistic expression. It brought me back to the days of my childhood, sewing cir-cus outfits abundant with fake rhinestones or painting bright wild flowers on handmade jewelry, when Mom's generous imagination poured out effortlessly, nourishing me with its richness. Unlike the Western world's constant emphasis on the rational left brain, the Balinese culture was a celebration of the instinctual right brain. We were immersed in a vital process of dance, theater, music, painting, wood carving, and mask making, not just as art forms but also as interpretations of life. We learned that creativity is so natural and widespread in Bali that there is no actual word in their language for art or artist. Rather, creativity is the natural means of honoring the gods and serving the community. Many women came home from Bali to take up forgotten passions of dance, piano, singing, painting, or poetry. I vowed to return to my love of writing.

Mom would have especially loved the seamless integration of art and spirituality. Every dance, shadow puppet, or theater performance was offered to one of the hundreds of Balinese gods and goddesses. Bali is the most diverse of all the Indonesian islands with Buddhism, Hinduism, and Islamism existing relatively well together. No one seemed to care whose god was being honored at any given event. One of my favorite enactments was the Barong dance in which a fantastic creature with bulging red eyes, giant fangs, and a massive black beard festooned with frangipani represents the eternal struggle between good and evil. The Barong creature is equally fierce and gentle, sad and joyful, and as his ancient tale unfolds I experience all the same contrasts within myself. In quintessential Balinese fashion neither side can win, because without a balance between good and evil the world would fall into chaos. This marvelous reconciliation of opposites was portrayed in every aspect of the island's culture, from its art to its agricultural methods—incorporating floods and drought as equal parts of the natural cycle—to its cuisine—adding both hot and cool spices to balance the lively flavors. It was as if at every turn we were reminded of the wisdom of the feminine, her invitation to embrace paradox rather than fight it, to find the partnership between opposites rather than pit them against each other.

The Balinese women offered us important lessons. They were stunning, delicate, and strong all at the same time. With honey-colored skin and ink-black hair down to their waists, they dressed in vibrant handmade batik wrapped tightly around their sensuous bodies. Though tiny and slender they carried teeming baskets of fruit or ceremonial offerings on their heads, walking for many miles through mountain roads and rough terrain. They breast-fed their children and raised them communal style with the whole village taking part. We learned firsthand how physically strong the women were during our dance classes. Balinese dance is subtle and complex, demanding high levels of strength and flexibility as an expression of the Balinese belief that physical balance creates inner spiritual balance.

Toward the end of our trip our Balinese sisters took us to the market place and helped us pick out brightly patterned batik in royal purple, tangerine, and peacock blue. They taught us how to wrap our sarongs and tie our sashes for the temple festival that we would attend the following day. Then our dance teacher Made showed us how to make temple offerings, skillfully demonstrating the intricate cuts and folds in a palm leaf until it formed a tiny green cradle held together with bamboo splinters.

"Now we place several grains of rice and a single flower of frangipani as offerings to the gods. And then you add your prayer." Her dazzling smile was her offering to us. It exuded grace and strength, the balance she had been teaching us all week in our dance lessons.

Sitting on the large porch of our bamboo house with the rushing sound of the river gorge below us, we silently followed Made's instructions as if we were already immersed in prayer. Soon we each held our temple offering. I felt I held all of Bali in that tiny green cradle; the seamless balance of the daily and the sacred, and the elegant synthesis of landscape, art, and spirituality all offered with heartfelt gratitude.

Elegantly wrapped in our sarongs and offerings in hand, we set out for the temple. For miles and miles the narrow dirt roads appeared as bright-colored streamers with each women's *banyar* (a village collective) in their particular sarong of turquoise, fuchsia, orange, chartreuse, or gold. Perched above the colors were the pyramid-shaped temple offerings, intricately built out of papayas, mangoes, avocados, eggs, and coconuts, and decorated with bundles of magenta orchids and scarlet hibiscus. Carrying the heavily laden offerings high on their heads, the tiny Balinese women glided along like a procession of vibrantly colored birds. Watching them, I longed to be able to carry my responsibilities with such grace and ease as an offering to spirit.

Arriving at the magnificent mother temple Pura Besakih, Made helped us find a place to sit on the stone floor. The only white faces in the crowd of hundreds of Balinese, the Straub *banyar* drew lots of attention and friendly smiles. This was the festival of Kuningan, and it was said that all the gods come down to earth on this day. Soon enough we understood why a god would leave heaven for this celebration. We sat mesmerized for about an hour before we would go up to the smaller temple within the temple to leave our offerings. The gamelan orchestras were heating up into a frenzy, reminding me of the untamed improvisational jazz heard in small clubs in New Orleans. Representing different characters from the great Hindu epic, the Ramayana, giant puppets on stilts walked among us. Clove incense was thick in the air, mixed with smell of human sweat and goats being slaughtered for temple offerings. Priests were praying in the complex Indonesian language, babies were crying, and all around people were talking and laughing. If it wasn't already abundantly clear that art, spirituality, and sensuality were intrinsically connected for the Balinese, then the temple festival proclaimed this one more time.

Later, Made helped us find our way to the inner temple, where we added our offerings dedicated to the sacred feminine to the heaping piles of those who had gone before us. We knew that after the gods have had their fill of the food's essence, the worshippers then take home the rest to their families. In this intoxicating celebration of life, I feel certain that the Goddess had heard our prayers. If ever there was a perfect opposite to the ordered monotonous Catholic mass of my childhood, it would be the Balinese temple festival. Thoroughly enjoying this orgy of the senses, I couldn't help but wonder what Mom would be feeling.

In my mountain valley home, on the bluestone fireplace at the very center of my hearth, stands a hand-carved wooden statue of the Balinese rice goddess Sri Dewa. Her body is both soft and fierce, her strong hands full of the earth, her heart open to the world, her face an invitation into the imagination. And her voice speaks a prayer that we may all take back the wisdom of the feminine.

Russia and the
Flying Women

Music

A flame burns within her, miraculously,
While you look, her edges crystallize.
She alone will draw near and speak to me
When others are afraid to meet my eyes.
She was with me even in my grave
When the last of my friends turned away,
And she sang like the first storm heaven gave,
Or as if flowers were having their say.
—Anna Akhmatova

I can't imagine a more stark contrast to the velvet breezes of
Bali than the winter winds of Moscow. But here I was in bit-
ter, snowy Moscow just months after returning from a trip to
Bali in 1992. I was sitting at the kitchen table of my dear friend
Zhenya Alexeeva drinking pot after pot of dark Russian tea

sweetened with gobs of red cherry jam. We were planning our training, called "The Deep Feminine: Russian Women's Empowerment." For the past three years David and I had collaborated with Zhenya to bring our empowerment process to Russia, but we had never done work just for women. After I shared with Zhenya some of my personal journey as well as the work I had been doing in Bali, she easily persuaded me to come back to Moscow. Now we were trying to figure out where to begin.

"Listen, Gail," Zhenya said urgently, her beautiful face full of concern. "You need to understand that it's a time of confusion and chaos in my country with the economy falling apart in front of our eyes. We see the rest of Eastern Europe in the midst of immense change and we Russians are afraid of being left behind. You already know how disempowered Russian women are and that there really isn't a woman's movement here to support us. And even though perestroika and glasnost are changing things here in Russia, life is still exceedingly hard for most Russian women. I don't even know where we can start with this workshop."

From meeting many women in our Moscow empowerment trainings I knew just how difficult life was for most Russian women. Though Father Lenin, as well as Father Gorbachev, had assured Russian women that they would become full partners in the new society, the patriarchs had forgotten about a few small details in the form of cooking, cleaning, washing, shopping, and tending and raising children. So now Russian women were expected to do it all: get married, raise a family, and have a full-time profession. Not to mention that in most homes men were not expected to help with the house or the children.

Taking more of the dark tea followed by the ubiquitous heaping teaspoons of cherry jam, I suggested that we start the training by letting women tell their stories in small groups, as we used to do in consciousness-raising groups in the sixties and seventies.

"Yes, okay," Zhenya nodded. "And maybe we could tell our own stories first to give the women courage and inspiration. And remember Gail, one of the reasons why your empowerment model works so well in the current climate in Russia is that it's not a dogma or a solution. We're teaching people that they are responsible for their own lives, and that they have to find their own way and answer their own questions. This is why empowerment is such an antidote to communism. And then, of course, is the real importance of teaching the women how to create a vision for their lives so they're not run by the fear of our society." Zhenya spoke about these ideas so matter of factly that I had to remind myself how visionary she was, and how much courage it took for her to introduce these innovative concepts to her Russian sisters. We had worked together enough times that I could tell that now she was on fire about our upcoming adventure. "At the end of the workshop, I'd like to sing some Russian folk songs about women."

Even though she had taught herself English only in the last several years, Zhenya spoke fluently and eloquently in her sonorous Russian accent. I loved her as a sister. She had an intensity and fearlessness that inspired me no end, and a poet's soul that was evident whenever she sang. I wasn't precisely sure what her folk songs meant, but I knew that Zhenya's singing would make a beautiful and meaningful ending.

Zhenya and I spent hours refining the training design. We created a guided journey where women could retrace their female lineage, getting wisdom from their mothers, grandmothers, and great-grandmothers. Using the format from my old consciousness-raising groups in Boston, we decided to teach the women exactly how to run their own support groups when they left the training. Many hours later, giddy with exhaustion and too much strong Russian tea, we began to reminisce about our friendship.

We remembered my first trip to Russia, when there was a sugar shortage in Moscow and I brought forty kilos of sugar in my suitcase. And during that first empowerment workshop some of the training words were so unusual that when our translator Igor couldn't find a Russian word he would just say the word in English very slowly, two or three times in a row. Then the whole room of a hundred people would start to laugh. And there was the memorable time the KGB agents came into our training and our gutsy colleague Yuri confronted them and kicked them out.

We both realized how many wonderful adventures we had shared. "And sad things too, dear Zhenya. Like the year that Gale was dying. If it weren't for Gale we wouldn't be sitting here together in your kitchen."

Our dear friend Gale Warner, an accomplished poet, journalist, and activist, had introduced Zhenya and me. Soon after that Gale found out that she had incurable lymphoma. She died at thirty, but not before she had finished her memoir, *Dancing at the Edge of Life*, which described the last year of her indomitable life.

"I know. I think of her all the time. I bet that Gale would be so happy with the training we are doing tomorrow."

And so it was on a snowy January morning at the venerable State Pedagogical Institute in the heart of Moscow that we dedicated our empowerment work for Russian women to our dear friend Gale Warner. Our training room was bright red with enormous high ceilings. Zhenya told me it used to be a chapel for young women but now the religious icons were replaced with plaster friezes of Marx and Lenin.

The women began to arrive from all over Russia. There were Natasha, Galina, Anya, Nadya, Olga, Sasha, Vera, Elena, and Irina, among others. How I loved the sound of their names. Zhenya and I greeted each of the seventy-five women with the gift of a long-stemmed red carnation. The big room was full to capacity and very full with the exuberance and longing of these Russian women.

Welcoming the women, we said how excited, and also nervous, we were about our two days together. I began by telling a fifteen-minute version of my life story with Natasha by my side, her melodious voice providing the simultaneous translation from English to Russian. I told of my family and childhood, about my mother and her early death and what that has meant in my life. I talked about my own betrayal of the feminine, my workaholism, and the constant cultural pressure to place reason over emotion, head over heart. When I described David and my choice not to have children there was an audible gasp in the room. A few minutes later I learned from the myriad of questions that this choice was unheard of in Mother Russia.

"How can you be a real woman and not have children?" asked a lively young Olga.

I was totally unprepared for the bewildered amazement that my choice had created. "Well," I started off, clearly flustered, "You see I am a woman and I am here." The Russian women began to laugh and I was relieved.

"But seriously, I think there are many ways to mother besides the traditional role. I bet that if some of you really believed you had the choice, you might decide not to have children. You might choose to dedicate your time to other worthy things like writing or research, working for social justice or the environment, or empowering the women in your country."

Now there was total pandemonium in the room. Seventy-five Russian women were talking and buzzing about choice and children, time and energy and dreams, and I was wondering

what Marx and Lenin up there on the walls must be thinking. Zhenya and I impulsively changed the training plan and
immediately put the women in small groups to tell their stories and talk about what choice really meant. Soon the room
was positively bursting with stories of joy and failure, marriage
and divorce, mothers and daughters, the merits and demer-
its of Russian men, the stress of careers in medicine, science,
politics, business, and grassroots activism. Peals of laughter
and tearful hugs abounded in every corner of the room. Lunch
was an hour late, but who cared. Hearts were open and ears
listened deeply; stories healed and opposites reconciled; ap-
propriate choice was as personal as each individual woman in
the room. This was the deep feminine in all her Russian glory.

At lunch we all placed our individual picnics on a big communal tablecloth on the floor, and I ate my first shiny orange
Russian kumquats. I settled in with Natasha for a winter picnic and conversation. "Life seems very hard here in Moscow.
Really, how do you manage, Natasha?"

"In Russia the external physical conditions are more difficult than in America but our interior lives are very rich in
imagination. We are extremely passionate on the inside. I
think the danger in your country is that your lives are so soft
and easy that you become spoiled and lazy inside." With perfect BBC English, her intense brown eyes drilled into me with
the words that I have never forgotten. Exquisite with her halo
of black curly hair surrounding her perfect alabaster skin and
her fierce intelligence, Natasha herself was the answer to my
question. As we continued to talk and enjoy the sweet and
sour kumquats, she helped me understand the sweet and sour
of America, the strange mixture of being simultaneously em-
ulated and despised. Through her penetrating Russian eyes I
could see how my culture's unmatched idealism was a blessing, but when this turned into arrogance it quickly became a

curse. This was 1991, a decade before the events of September 11, 2001, and unbeknownst to dear Natasha she was giving me advance warning.

When lunch was over we settled in to hear some of the stories in the large group. Galina began. "I am twenty-eight and married with two small children. I work full-time as a research scientist. I live with my husband's family. Last week when I came home from work, I saw that my only bottle of perfume was empty and my mother-in-law was passed out drunk on the couch. If we live with my family, it's even worse because of my mother's depression since we lost my father under Stalin. I am exhausted all the time with my job and my children, and I don't have anything left for my marriage or myself."

As Galina spoke I thought of my mother and the exhaustion that ate her alive. I realized that many of these Russian women were living my mother's reality. Later I told them how grateful I was that they had given me new ways to appreciate my mother's life. Then, hearing more women's stories, we all began to feel the strength that comes from careful listening and the incomparable medicine that comes from telling the truth and having it witnessed. In this ancient ritual of give and take the deep feminine was running through us with her sure currents of collaboration and inclusiveness. Her nonhierarchal wisdom was apparent as our stories taught that we were all equal in the territory of the human heart.

Now Zhenya told her story of a painful divorce and her new marriage to handsome Volodya. She described her own struggles of mothering her two strong daughters, Dasha and Vera. As she talked about her passion for Russian music and poetry and how these arts provided the spiritual foundation for her daughters, I felt deeply moved. Then she turned to her professional life as a physician and told us how she left her work as a doctor to become the founder of the organization Golubka, dedicated to bringing personal and social empowerment to Russia. I felt so proud of her as I listened to her story through Natasha's whispered translation. A decade later Zhenya would become the founder of yet another visionary endeavor, the first of its kind in Russia, educating people about AIDS and HIV. Having created a balance between a rich interior life and a passionate engagement with the world, my Russian sister was a living example of an empowered woman.

When she finished her story, Zhenya said she would like to sing a Russian folk song called "Flying Woman." Since I wouldn't understand the words in Russian, she translated for me first. "Flying woman, you have two burdens, hard work during the day and taking care of crying children at night. You feel your life has broken your wings. But remember you can still fly above the clouds. You are flying woman."

Zhenya took up her guitar and began the song, her voice pure and powerful, the Russian language never so plaintive. I fell in love with her all over again and I remembered the final line of Anna Akhmatova's poem "Music": "And she sang like the first storm heaven gave / Or as if flowers were having their say." I looked around the room at all these resplendent Russian women. I saw that we had remembered that we could still fly above the clouds. We were, indeed, flying women.

China

Black Birds Against a White Sky

The mystery of the valley is immortal;
It is known as the Subtle Female.
The gateway of the Subtle Female
Is the source of Heaven and Earth.

Everlasting, endless, it appears to exist.
Its usefulness comes with no effort.

—Lao Tzu

I left Moscow and my dear friend Zhenya deeply inspired. On the long flight back home to New York, I thought about my life and what was next for me. I took out the traditional hand-painted *matryoshka* doll that Zhenya had given me as a gift. *Matryoshka* means "mother" in Russian. Placing all six of the bright blue, yellow, and red Russian nesting dolls on my airplane tray, I understood something.

In working with women, in surrounding myself with their stories and their wisdom, both my story and my mother's story were being reshaped. Now my mother's story had been touched by the artistry of Bali and her spirit was held in the strong loving arms of many Russian women. Bali's landscape and Made's presence, Zhenya, Natasha, and Galina had all mothered me by helping me to understand who I was as a woman. As we placed one another's stories into our hearts, they changed us and became part of us. Our stories were nested in one another.

The Russian women, especially in their reaction to my decision not to have children, had inspired me to think deeply about choice. How do we really choose our own lives? Like me, how many women were living their mother's unlived life? Or, their father's version of life? How do we find the balance of freedom and responsibility in choosing our lives? These questions were at the very heart of reclaiming the conscious feminine. Thinking about all of this, I knew I wanted to go back to China and work with my friend Kitty Xia. I wanted to find out how Chinese women thought about choice and to find out how their stories were part of me.

Through my work with the First Earth Run I had met the diminutive Kitty Xia when she served as my translator on my first trip to China in 1986. Falling in love with China, her vast history and immense territory, her personality such a vital contrast to America, I returned many times in my role as a citizen diplomat. On one of my trips I brought the first citizen delegation into China after the 1989 Tiananmen Square crisis. Another time my delegation of citizen diplomats met with Jiang Zemin when he was still the mayor of Shanghai, before rising to the heights of premier of China. Other trips included symposiums with Chinese scholars of Confucius and Lao Tzu, lessons in calligraphy and Chinese landscape painting, qigong and Dunhuang boxing. During these trips I had covered thousands of miles from Beijing to Xi'an to Kunming, from Guilin to Shanghai to Jinan and all the way to Harbin, crisscrossing China in trains, planes, buses, and on foot.

Throughout most of these miles, Kitty Xia had accompanied me as my translator. She had served as translator to a long list of luminaries including Richard Nixon, Billy Graham, and the Beatles. I couldn't believe my good fortune to have her as both my friend and translator. She and I had happily agreed that if I were Chinese I would like to be Kitty, and if she were American she would like to be me.

Once Kitty had confided in me that her boss didn't approve of her traveling so much with me because I was not an important person. "But I lied to him," she said with a burst of her exuberant high-pitched laughter, "and told him you actually were a very important person. Because, to tell the truth, your trips are more fun than the diplomats' boring official visits. They are so interesting I wouldn't want to miss them." Again came her unique laugh that I loved so much.

I adored Kitty. She was bright, irreverent, and ingenious at outsmarting the never-ending bureaucratic red tape in China. She was adept at working the *guangxi*, the old boy's network, even though she was one of the few women in her department at the Foreign Affairs Office. When I suggested the idea of a delegation of American women meeting with Chinese women to discuss women's empowerment, she went to work immediately to help make the trip possible.

Back at home I was busy preparing the American delegation. With the help of my friend Roxanne Lanier, who had already traveled to China with me, we got a small Rockefeller grant to help fund our trip. In May 1992, our delegation of psychologists, psychotherapists, professors, anthropologists, poets, and writers gathered in Roxanne's elegant living room in San Francisco for our orientation. Having been immersed in the planning stages of our trip for eight months, now for the first time we were all together. My friend's living room was bursting with the excitement of ten women all talking at once about the thrill of leaving for China in a few hours. In boisterous conversations we reviewed some of the details of our carefully prepared presentations for the Chinese Women's Federation, including sessions on empowerment, dream work, the use of intuition in healing, psychodrama, and the role of meditation in modern life. For months we had been reading about China, studying elementary Chinese, listening to Chinese classical music, and now we could barely wait to get on the plane to Beijing.

Kitty was waiting for us at the Beijing Airport and I was overjoyed to see her. She was dressed in China red and her long black ponytail gave her an eternally girlish look. Soon we were on our bus, riding through the teeming streets of Beijing along with hundreds and hundreds of bicycles. We passed wide-open parks with large crowds doing t'ai chi or qigong and people flying giant kites shaped like butterflies, monkeys, and dragons. The pungent smell of Chinese spices wafted up from the small food stands on every corner, mixed with the choppy staccato sound of the Chinese language. All around us we were enveloped by bright brown eyes and shiny black hair. Immediately I had the same sensation I always did when I arrived in China: the feeling of being swallowed up by a culture that vast and ancient, and so different from my own. As an American I loved this unusual feeling of smallness being encompassed by this Chinese largeness.

Kitty gave my delegation an entertaining and enlightening orientation in her flawless English. "First it's important to know that our sense of time is very different than yours. By understanding this you can appreciate some of the most important cross-cultural differences between our countries. We Chinese do not have the sense of urgency you do. You Americans are always in a hurry, feeling you have to get things done right now. Because of our four-thousand-year-old history, we Chinese have a very protracted and telescopic sense of time. This gives us a lot of patience, which you Americans certainly don't have," she said, smiling coyly at the group.

I had heard her give this overview before and it was such a demonstration of Kitty's brilliance and lively humor. She continued, "It's also very important to remember that there are two totally different societies in China, almost like two different cultures. There's the urban intellectual society in our big cities, and then eighty percent of China is the rural peasant society. The peasants don't like the intellectuals and feel that they are greedy, impractical, and out of touch with reality. And the intellectuals feel the peasants are behind the times. This pervading tension keeps us all on our toes." Kitty started to laugh, her face folded in joy, telling us how much she loved the phrase "keeps us on our toes" because it was untranslatable in Chinese.

"Above all, remember, ladies, we Chinese are still absorbed with the ancient concept of the Middle Kingdom. That is, we still consider ourselves at the center of the world and superior to the rest of the world. And so you see, in a paradoxical way we Chinese and you Americans are more alike than you might think. Here's a phrase I want you to remember—'the Chinese are ethnocentric and the Americans are egocentric.'" Her eloquence was followed by her trademark high-pitched laugh.

After several days of exploring the cultural marvels at the Temple of Heaven, the Summer Palace of the Empress Dowager, the tombs of the Ming emperors, the Great Wall of China, and the Beijing Opera, the women in my delegation started to really feel China. Allowing this vast ancient culture to engulf them, they were initiated into how young and small America is from a global perspective. For some of the women, this realization in itself was life changing, adding a vital perspective that far too few Americans ever gain.

Now it was time for our meetings with the Chinese Women's Federation of Beijing. One of the largest women's organizations in the world, with thousands of members and hundreds of chapters throughout the vast territory of China, the federation's purpose is to promote all aspects of women's social welfare. The Beijing Women's Federation is housed in an elegant building on the tree-columned Tai Ji Chang Street. Greeting us at the door was the tiny Mrs. Li Gangzhong. A woman in her mid-sixties, Mrs. Li had the vitality of a thirty-year-old. I had already had the honor of working with her on several other occasions, and I knew she had more titles than could fit on her business card: Chairman, Women's Federation of Beijing; President, Foundation for Children's Welfare; president, Beijing Society for the Study of Theory Concerning Women's Problems; and so on.

This petite lady with her towering presence led us into a spacious room with sunlight and fresh air pouring in from abundant wide windows. Our Chinese colleagues were waiting for us. There we were, ten American women and ten Chinese women. At first we were all shy, wondering how our days together would go. But soon enough, after rounds of fragrant jasmine tea and traditional sweets accompanied by Kitty's impeccable translation and infectious laugh, we began to relax.

Li had invited her colleague Mrs. Zhao, a calligraphy master, to give us a demonstration that she felt would take us into the very essence of the Chinese culture. Before beginning, Mrs. Zhao spoke quietly. "I have studied calligraphy for fifty years, starting when I was five years old. But I am still only learning my craft." We all felt that rarest of humility that comes with mastery. In that beautiful room with the tall wood-paneled windows framed by delicate lace curtains lifting with the breeze, Zhao spread her rolls of rice paper across the table and placed her brushes and ink by her side. Calm yet deeply focused, she began to form the ancient Chinese characters, each a meditation unto itself, each a black bird in flight against a white sky. Utterly silent but for the sound of Zhao's brush against the rice paper, so complete was our concentration that soon it was as if we too were an extension of her brush, we too were the black birds flying across her white sky.

Soon the smell of Zhao's ink transported me back to the kitchen table at Brecks Lane, where I would watch Mom as she did her ink sketches for newspaper ads for the local women's stores. After hanging the actual bright silk and linen dresses on our old brown refrigerator so she could see them well, she spread several kinds of paper, pencils, art gum, inks, and various sharp pen tips in front of her. Sketching in heavy dark pencil, she would transfer the image onto translucent paper by rubbing over the sketch, then creating the final product in black ink. Her sketches were as intricate and precise as any photograph. Now, watching Zhao, I remembered exactly how the tips of my mother's fingers would stay black for days from the ink stains and how much I loved that. I don't know which moved me more that afternoon, Zhao's consummate craft or the warm memory of Mom happily immersed in her sketches.

As in Bali and Russia, it was the stories we women exchanged that opened us up and lodged in our hearts. Our Chinese counterparts were brave young visionaries. Wei Wei had started one of the first rape crisis hotlines in China. Gao was instrumental in organizing counseling centers for university students, and other Chinese sisters were integrating modern Western psychological models with ancient Chinese practices like acupuncture and qigong.

On our final day during a lively discussion on the need for female ingenuity in the midst of a man's world, Mrs. Li told us a wonderful story. "About ten years ago," Li began, "I became aware of the high infant mortality rate here in Beijing. I set up a committee to study this and we found that in many cases pregnant women in labor were not getting to the hospital on time. Over ninety percent of our women rely on buses or bicycles for transportation and these modes of travel weren't efficient enough for a woman with labor complications. I went about the normal government channels to see if more ambulances or police cars could be used. But after months I wasn't getting anywhere and I knew I was stuck in endless bureaucratic red tape. So I took matters in my own hands, as we say.

"I decided to start my own taxi company just for women in labor. I gathered together women friends who could help me raise the money to buy a fleet of taxis. Soon we had a fleet of your old American yellow cabs from the 1950s. We decided all the drivers would be women and in many cases nurses. Before you knew it, everyone in Beijing knew about our unique Women's Taxi Company. We have saved many lives, both mothers and babies. Now there are taxi companies like this in many other parts of China." She beamed. "I love this story because it is a woman's empowerment story, isn't it, Gail?"

"I would say so, Li!" Both the Chinese and the American women were equally moved by Li's combination of ingenuity, determination, and courage. She was offering us such precious teaching about women's leadership.

Later that afternoon I presented the empowerment support group model that I had taught for many years. Explaining the exact format and sharing some of the guiding principles such as rotating facilitation, deep listening, clear safe guidelines that encourage trust and vulnerability, respect for differences, and balanced attention to process and outcome, I had found that these concepts were often a confirmation of women's natural leadership instincts. To underscore how the process worked I shared a variety of stories from women's support groups in Russia, America, and Europe who had used the model successfully.

"It's so simple, this idea of supporting one another," I said. "What's often the most difficult is asking for support. So often when we're in the most trouble, the dark night of the soul, we retreat and isolate ourselves. If the support group is well set up and we keep an eye on one another, then when someone is in trouble she doesn't fall off the radar screen. Of course this wasn't so necessary in our grandmother's time, before our neighborhoods and communities had fallen apart. And perhaps because you are far more communal in China than we are in America, you still take care of one another more than we do?" I asked.

Mrs. Li spoke up immediately with a seriousness I hadn't seen before. "Yes, it's true that we Chinese are less individualistic than you Americans, and I think you can learn from us in that regard. But culturally we are not encouraged to share difficult times or to ask for support. We Chinese are very stoic, sometimes too stoic. The whole time you have been speaking I have been sitting here with a heavy heart. Two months ago my dearest woman friend committed suicide." Li paused and began to quietly, almost silently, weep. Indeed everyone in the room was now crying.

As tears ran down my cheeks I thought of my Grandpa Straub's suicide and my father's stoicism. Only once, when we were all sitting at the kitchen table during a big fight between my parents, had my father mentioned the time during the Great Depression when his own father put a gun to his head while Pop and his mother stood watching. The Chinese translation for stoicism is "to eat bitter." All his life my father had eaten bitter but it wasn't until that moment, in that room in Beijing, that I understood the full impact of his stoicism on my life. I saw both his nobility and courage and the way his stoicism had repressed his feelings and led to emotional distance. Finally I could see how that distance had made it impossible for me to discuss Grandpa Straub's suicide as my father was dying. Perhaps now I could forgive both my father and myself.

As I wept for so many people, Li continued to astonish me. "As we have already discussed today, though the government tries to conceal this, the suicide rate in China is among the highest in the world. This was especially true during the Cultural Revolution. I would like to think if my dear friend had believed she could ask for help, perhaps she would be sitting with us today. I would like to bring this support group model to all our chapters in the Women's Federation of China."

I have never witnessed a more dignified and elegant female power than that of Mrs. Li Gangzhong. Dressed in a high-collared traditional Chinese silver gown, she was luminous in her vulnerability, her intelligence, and her fierce commitment to social justice. I wanted every woman in the world to meet her. I wanted her to be my Chinese mother.

We ended our final day together with our favorite poems or literary passages. Annie Dillard, Emily Dickinson, and Maya Angelou were mixed with passages from Tsao Hsueh-chin's *Dream of the Red Chamber* and Shen Rong's *At Middle Age*. After a while Kitty said it was too hard to translate such great literature and we just listened to the pure sound of the Chinese or English. When it was Kitty's turn, she shared a poem from one of China's greatest women poets, the twelfth-century Zhou Xuanjing.

> Meditating at midnight,
> Meditating at noon,
> A mind like autumn
> Comes to the Way's deep heart.
> Under motionless waves,
> Fish and dragons freely leap.
> In the sky without limits,
> Only the moonlight stays.

And as a sign of honor, Mrs. Li went last. "I would like to end with a passage from Lao Tzu, because I know how Gail and her husband David love the teachings of this great Chinese master. I have chosen this passage because it is so relevant to the topics we have been discussing today. I will read it first in Chinese and then in English."

Perceiving the Subtle

The mystery of the valley is immortal;
It is known as the Subtle Female.
The gateway of the Subtle Female
Is the source of Heaven and Earth.

Everlasting, endless, it appears to exist.
Its usefulness comes with no effort.

As Li read the passage from the Tao, I saw so clearly that Lao Tzu's teachings are all about the feminine. The Tao is the way of the receptive, that mysterious power leading to a fluency between the visible and the invisible worlds. Its power comes from its subtle imagination and lack of force. And Mrs. Li, my Chinese mother, was a living example of the way of the Tao.

Sitting in that lovely room on Tai Ji Chang Street with Li's voice reciting the Tao in Chinese, I found myself thinking of my own mother. I wanted her to be touched by Li's presence. I longed for her to know that we don't have to betray our feminine wisdom in order to be strong.

After a sumptuous banquet of chicken, beef, octopus, squid, and Peking duck, all accompanied by the haunting strains of Chinese classical music and nonstop girl talk with our Chinese sisters, we staggered back to our hotel so full on every level I was ready to collapse. But the day was not over yet.

As I was getting into the elevator, Kitty said she needed to speak to me. "Of course, Kitty, should we sit in the bar?"

"No," she said. "I need someplace private. Let's go to my room."

I readily agreed, wondering what on earth Kitty wanted to talk about at this hour after a day like ours. Once we had settled in on Kitty's bed she began in earnest. "Gail, today was very emotional for me. Because I am the translator I cover my emotions under my professionalism. But the women's stories really got to me and I need to tell you more of my own story." My Chinese sister's lovely face was filled with uncharacteristic sadness, revealing the parts of her that lay just beneath her brilliance and humor.

"Of course, Kitty, what do you need to tell me?" I was now completely wide awake. "Can I make you a nice cup of jasmine tea before you begin?"

"No, no tea, I just want to talk. I have told you some of these things before, Gail. You know that I lost my father in the Cultural Revolution because of his political ideas. And my brother, a prominent physicist, was forced to leave and go to America or he, too, would probably have lost his life. And some members of my extended family did commit suicide during that awful time. I was left to care for my mother, Old Cat. I have always put caring for Old Cat first and then my career next. So I am not married and I don't have children. This is very unusual in China." Kitty said sadly, holding back her tears. "I guess I am just an old maid."

Overwhelmed by tenderness for my friend but respecting our cultural differences, I resisted my American temptation to take her in my arms and hold her. I, too, held back my tears and simply took her hand in mine and asked, "Do you want to get married, dear Kitty?"

"I have never met a man I could fall in love with and I am too old and too modern to have an arranged marriage. And I love how interesting my life is. I like the people from all over the world that I meet and how much I get to travel. I like to serve my country through my work. It's just that there is so much pressure on a woman to marry and have children. I am really an odd goose here in China, Gail."

"You mean odd duck," I said gently, correcting my dear friend's English and realizing yet again how unique and brave, and especially how far ahead of her generation, she was. "You know, Kitty, my mother, Jacquie, made the opposite choice from you. She was a gifted artist and she gave up her career to marry and have a family. I know she had regrets about this and it was part of what broke her heart. And as her daughter I have partly built my life as an answer to my mother's unfulfilled dreams. Perhaps your life is an answer to Old Cat's life?"

Kitty began to cry. "I've never thought of it that way, but I think it's true. Except for me, Old Cat lost her whole family during the Cultural Revolution. If I had left her to live with a husband or a husband's family it would have broken her heart. And I don't think there was room for any more heartbreak in Old Cat's life. My mother is very proud of me. I share the stories of all of my adventures with her and it's almost like she is living them with me."

And now I began to cry. "Kitty, how I would have loved to share my adventures with my mother. She was so young when she died that she didn't see any of my life. It's so hard to know if I have made the right choices, choices my mother would be proud of. I've finally decided that with any choice we both gain and lose. You and I, Old Cat and Jacquie, we all gained something and we all lost something. Maybe the destiny between mothers and daughters is the exchange of these unlived parts." Saying all this through my tears, I once again had that special feeling that transpires when my own life story is being reshaped by its intersection with another woman's story. In that moment I understood that part of conscious choice is the willingness to embrace the paradox of what is gained and what is lost.

And then Kitty, my self-contained Chinese sister, took me in her arms and said with such sweetness, "Your mother would be so proud of you, Gail. I don't want you ever to wonder about that again. And I have an idea. Would you like to meet Old Cat tomorrow? I want you to share your life adventures with my mother." Her impish grin was never more winning.

"My dear Kitty, I would love nothing more than to meet Old Cat."

And so it was that Old Cat, Kitty, and I met for tea the next day in one of Beijing's most famous teahouses. Looking out on a Chinese rock garden framed by weeping willows, we sat in an ancient courtyard surrounded by pots of large-petaled pink lotus flowers. Over heaping servings of steamed dumplings Kitty insisted that I tell Old Cat all about my life. As the tiny old Chinese woman dressed in black silk cooled herself with a sandalwood fan, her daughter's flawless translation wove the story of my childhood, Mom's illness and death during my years in Africa, my hippie days, and right up to my father's death as the crisis that brought my mother alive again.

Really all I wanted that afternoon was to lose myself in Old Cat's face, a face that told not only her story but also China's story. She didn't know exactly how old she was but she guessed in her late seventies or early eighties. Looking into her eyes I felt such pain and tender compassion, I saw a treasure map of China's telescopic sense of time and human suffering, informing my young American psyche about fatalism and patience. Encoded in the wisdom of Old Cat's face I saw my Grandma Walsh with nine children; I saw Grammie Straub just after Grandpa Straub's suicide and how strong my father was for his mother; and I saw my mother's dreams intertwined with mine in a double helix, a reconciliation of opposites.

As the bright afternoon faded into early evening dusk, we said our goodbyes and Old Cat reminded me that for the Chinese one of the most important things in life is to honor your ancestors and to show the greatest respect for the history that has come before you. You must honor your mother's memory and you must learn from your past, she told me as her unforgettable visage made a permanent imprint on my heart. At that moment Old Cat became the archetype of China, encapsulating what we had all learned on this trip about time and history, suffering and resilience, individualism and community. Her parting words to me offered not just the wisdom that I needed, but also the wisdom that our youth-obsessed, shortsighted American culture needs. And with her goodbye, Old Cat firmly and tenderly planted the first seed in me to write a book to honor my mother.

Pilgrimage to Ireland

Shape Shifting

I have been in many shapes before I attained
    this form.
I have been a drop in the air,
I have been a shining star,
A bridge for passing over three score rivers.
I have journeyed as an eagle,
A boat on the sea.
I have been many things . . .
         —Taliesin, sixth-century Celtic poet

I had traveled far away from home to learn from the women in
Bali and Russia and China. Now our stories were braided together, forming an ancient pattern in which we were all one
another's mothers, daughters, and sisters, and we all helped
one another understand who we were as women. Interwoven,
our differences and our commonalities formed the foundation
for our role as global citizens. The words from Maya Angelou's
poem "Human Family" had become a living reality for me:
"We are more alike, my friends, than we are unalike."

In witnessing these varied stories from all over the world I came to understand that the conscious feminine embraced all choices. It honored women who stayed home with their children, women who raised children and worked, and women like me who chose not to have children and were mothering in nontraditional ways. Intrinsic to the very nature of the feminine was a spacious womb that had room for diversity on all levels: lifestyle, politics, faith, and ethnicity. The core essence of female wisdom was its nonhierarchal respect for diversity and complexity, reversing the simplistic dominant worldview of right and wrong, black and white, powerful and not powerful. My sisters around the globe had placed this wisdom at the very center of my being, making it the heartbeat of my existence.

My global sisters had also prepared me to return to my mother's roots in Ireland. Now I was ready to make a pilgrimage to her homeland. My last pilgrimage crossing the Sahara had taken place less than a year after my mother's death. That journey had left me burying my real feelings of grief and loss rather than awakening the truth inside me. When I left Africa and the Sahara, I crossed an invisible line back into the Western world of rational thinking, mind over heart, masculine over feminine. Twenty-one years later as I made my way to Ireland, I had grieved my mother and I had taken back my female wisdom. I wanted this trip to be a pilgrimage in the true sense of the word, a journey during which I left the safe parameters of my daily routine. I hoped that this time, as I allowed myself to be turned upside down, I would return home stronger and truer. I loved the theologian Richard Niebuhr's description of a person on a pilgrimage: "Pilgrims are persons in motion—passing through territories not their own—seeking something we might call completion, or perhaps the word clarity will do as well, a goal to which only the spirit's compass points the way."

With my spirit's compass I set out for Ireland searching
for some sort of clarity or completion with my mother. Ac-
companying me on my pilgrimage were four of my closest
friends, Gunilla, Ro, Ellen, and Danit. These four darlings
were my women's group, and we called ourselves the Helix
Sisters, in honor of the double helix symbol representing a
reconciliation of opposites. Auspiciously, we had met at a
learning center in New York City called Women and Wisdom. My Helix Sisters had mothered me, witnessed me, and,
at the time of this trip, put up with me for more than fifteen
years. We knew one another's stories intimately—the good,
the bad, the sad, and the funny. We were an odd mix of Russian Jewish, Swedish, German, and Irish heritage going off to
the land of the Celts. Gunilla, the eldest, is a poet, healer,
and Renaissance woman whose books help people find the
sacred in daily living. Ro is a gifted psychotherapist and activist living the quintessential creative life in Santa Fe. Ellen
is a courageous pioneering consultant working to bring the
feminine into the corporate sector. Danit is a visionary healer
and one of the wisest, funniest people I know.

We five see ourselves as a living experiment in the conscious feminine. True to our Helix name, we are a blending of
opposites. Some of us live quietly and simply, while others gal-
lop around the world. We are both gay and straight, fitness buffs
and couch potatoes, having lots of money and just enough
money. Several of us find utter pleasure from the most Zen experiences, while others prefer sumptuous luxury. We hail from
five different states stretching from Vermont to New Mexico
and we have agreed that it doesn't make practical sense for us
to meet on a regular basis, nor would we likely be friends if we
met one another on the street. Indeed, there is absolutely nothing rational about this group of sisters. But whenever we come
together, as we have now three times a year for more than

twenty-five years, utter magic happens. The regal irrational, queen of the divine feminine, rules on high as we laugh and fight and heal one another. We are loving and bitchy and silly and wise with one another. Recounting our unfolding life stories, we each have the privilege of four strong individuals offering counsel as a unified whole, four aspects of a shimmering holograph of female wisdom. The richness of our friendship comes from each particular woman as well as the whole that we make together. I imagine us as sage crones, most likely sitting in comfortable wicker rocking chairs by the sea, still delving into the inexplicable mysteries of our womanhood.

You can understand why there were no other four people with whom I would have made this pilgrimage. We arrived in Ireland in June when everything was in full blossom and the green of the countryside dazzled us. Hedges of wild red fuchsia, bundles of yellow irises, and sprays of purple heather and hollyhock blanketed the hillsides in glorious patterns. Like Bali, Ireland was a place where landscape, art, and spirituality lived in close relationship. With this holy trinity guiding the way, we five Helix Sisters were in heaven exploring stone circles, wedge graves, standing stones, and holy wells. Among the ancient Celtic sites we visited were Uragh, Leitrim Beg, and Cashelkeelty, which legend said marked the entrances to the underworld where the Tuatha de Danaan, or the little people, lived. The veil was thin and we were open to radical surprises.

One of those radical surprises was our encounter with John O'Donohue, Irish scholar and poet and, at the time, still a Catholic priest. The brilliant and irreverent Mr.O'Donohue was much more druid than priest. One fine day he took the Helix Sisters hiking to St. Patrick's Bed, high in the Cashel Mountains. Picnics packed, we set out to spend the full day walking through the untamed beauty of Conamara. We hiked quietly as close friends can do, without any need to fill up the rare stillness with talk. Occasionally John would pause at a striking rock formation, speaking to us in his marvelous way. "Have you noticed that the landscape lives mainly in silence? And though it is always watching us, it rarely intrudes. I sometimes think that these stones are praising the silence."

Soon, I had the distinct feeling that John was saying a mass in this vast cathedral of the Cashels. Each stop we made was like a stop at the stations of the cross, reminding me of when Mom used to pray the stations every Friday at St. Joseph's Church. I had brought my mother's old black rosary beads and now I took them out and fingered the beads that she had held so often with such reverence. John came to the next bend in the upward winding trail and spoke again. "The landscape is so generous, so patient, and hospitable to us. How is it we can abuse and rape it? What do you suppose happens to our inner landscape when we have raided our outer landscape?" Leaving us to contemplate his unsettling question, he led us onward toward St. Patrick's Bed, and we soon arrived at the enormous stone outcropping that looked like a giant's spacious resting place.

Sweating from our strenuous climb, we lay silently on our backs on the saint's limestone bed. Enraptured with the wild and ever-changing Irish sky, I watched the clouds rush about like crowds in a frenzied hurry. Soon the warm rain swept through, like a gentle traffic cop, clearing the chaos and ushering in a dazzling, cornflower blue sky. Showing me its venerable cycle of chaos, cleansing, and clarity, the Irish sky offered valuable teaching. As we ate our picnics of thick Irish brown bread and savory local goat's cheese, I spoke with John about my Catholic upbringing and my inability to reconcile my strong feminist beliefs with the patriarchal views of the Church. "I am devoted to my Buddhist meditation practice. But it's very impersonal and I miss the intimacy of prayer. I think I really miss Mother Mary," I said, surprised at my own words.

"Ah, well then," he said in his irresistible Conamara brogue, "Gail, you must take back Mary and leave the parts of the Church that don't seem genuine to you." Though he didn't realize it, John's words had a profound effect on me, allowing me to reclaim aspects of my Catholic roots in a way that made sense to me. Ever since that day in the Cashel Mountains, I have returned to my love of the Mother Mary, praying the rosary daily and very often when I walk. Whenever I want or need to pray I immediately turn to Mary.

As we devoured our dark chocolate bars, John continued his probing questions. "What is it, Gail, that allows you to feel most alive, and most in touch with the divine imagination?" Using his wonderful term for God, the druid Irishman was asking me to define my spiritual worldview. Here I was, sitting on St. Patrick's Bed, having just taken the Mother Mary back, and now I was being asked to articulate my cosmology. "I think this pilgrimage is working," I thought, laughing at the loveliness of it all.

"Being in the natural world has always felt holy to me. Silence and prayer nourish me a lot, though it's hard to find as much time for that as I would like."

John replied that one of the greatest traps for modern seekers is the perceived lack of time for spiritual practice. And we both agreed that silence was like an endangered species, an irreplaceable fundamental that we had to protect it at all costs.

"Sometimes," I mused, "I feel the presence of the sacred most directly when I am serving other people. That's why I love my work so much. And I am very blessed to be part of a vibrant community back home in Woodstock."

Talking with John that day, I could see that though I was a lapsed Catholic, I did have a rich relationship with the divine imagination. What I didn't know sitting there on Conamara's million-year-old limestone was that those very aspects of the sacred which I had just described—silence, landscape, service, and inquiry into cosmology—would become the foundations for my work as a spiritual mother.

Happy and spent after our hike, we visited with John's mother, Josie O'Donohue, who served us strong tea and warm scones as we sat next to the peat fire. As Josie spoke with her strong Irish accent, I pictured my Grandma Walsh in this very kitchen, with her nine children traipsing about. That night back at our country house on the shores of Cashel Bay, I lay in my bed smelling the sea mingled with the rose gardens just outside my window. I read one of John's poem's, which he had written for Josie. It was called "Beannacht," the word for "blessing" in Gaelic. By the third verse I began to weep as I thought of Mom.

When the canvas frays
in the currach of thought
and a stain of ocean
blackens beneath you,
may here come across the waters
a path of yellow moonlight
to bring you safely home.

May the nourishment of the earth be yours,
may the clarity of light be yours,
may the fluency of the ocean be yours,
may the protection of the ancestors be yours.

And so may a slow
wind work these words
of love around you,
an invisible cloak
to mind your life.

In the solitude of my room I longed to read the poem aloud and offer this blessing to my mother, as if she were sitting next to me. I wanted to tell Jacquie Walsh that I had held her old black rosary beads as I sat on St. Patrick's Bed, and that I had taken back the Mother Mary today. I had felt Grandma Walsh's presence in Josie's kitchen. I wanted her to know that I had met a druid priest named John O'Donohue who helped me be at home with my eclectic sense of the sacred, and that some years later John would be booted out of the Catholic Church because his views were too radical, too real, and too empowering. But, unlike her, John did not spend an inordinate amount of his life petitioning the Church or trying to be accepted back into the fold in order to please a God whose narrow rules strangle the spirit out of you. Rather, he became a poet and writer, a scholar who helped thousands of people in many corners of the globe to celebrate the infinite faces of the divine. Here, my dear mother, I offer you John's example as my *beannacht* to you.

There were many more things, things I didn't even know of yet, that I wanted to say to my mother. But I was just halfway through my pilgrimage and other radical surprises were waiting for me. As we left Conamara for County Cork in the southwest of Ireland, all five of us continued to fall under the county's mystical spell. During the day we hiked the untamed land, visiting ancient Celtic holy sites. As we Helix Sisters did whenever we were together, we created our own simple rituals to mark the important passages of our lives. At stone circles we honored what had come full circle within us and at wedge graves what needed to die. Standing stones allowed us to reflect on what part of us was standing tall, and at holy wells we pondered what might be hidden deep down inside us.

Later, in the long northern light of Irish nights, we ate like mother bears the freshest lobster, prawns, oysters, wild salmon, and trout. When we were able to stagger over to a local pub we were rewarded with the astonishing vitality of the Celtic music renaissance. Harps, fiddles, and frame drums, pipes, low whistles, and accordions were played superbly by men and women of all ages who were plumbers, carpenters, and nurses by day. One fine night our Irish friends talked us into learning a complicated traditional jig. Mercifully, we had imbibed enough Guinness. I shall never forget the sight of five Helix Sisters kicking and twirling and prancing across the rough wooden pub floor as if we had lived in Ireland all our lives.

Having spent enough time with one another, we knew how to carefully balance our time together with solitary pilgrimage. Through various misunderstandings over the years, we had learned that some of us were introverts and needed time alone to find replenishment, while others who were extroverts found their rejuvenation in jovial shopping trips in pursuit of handwoven sweaters and shawls. As long as we understood who needed what, we were fine. I was one of the Helix Sisters who needed my solitude or I became grouchy and withdrawn. During one such time I started out with a small knapsack and journal to spend the afternoon alone walking through the countryside. As I had before on this journey, I experienced my hiking as prayer, awed as I was by the diverse splendor of the creation. Walking deep into the Irish fields of sheep and jagged stone walls, I came across a wild fruit tree in full bloom. Its white blossoms were like a fragrant cloud floating in the midst of the verdant fields. As I approached the tree I saw a round opening in the ground, like a small womb or cave in the earth, roomy enough for me to lie down. I went into the grassy opening and lay down to rest with the blue sky ceiling above me.

No sooner had I closed my eyes than I experienced my mother's presence next to me, clearer than I had felt her

since her death more than twenty years before. I felt an overwhelming sadness for all the things we would never share.
First and foremost was my husband David, who was now so
much a part of me that Mom's not knowing him seemed almost incomprehensible. I mourned her not ever knowing my
work in the world and the rich and meaningful life that she
had helped inspire. I felt my loss that she had never visited
my beloved mountain home and met my close community of
friends who would have loved her. My grief poured forth as I
lay on the very ground of my mother's heritage. When I finally opened my eyes, I saw piles of bones in the corners of
the earth cave where I lay. White bones surrounded by white
blossoms from the wild fruit tree.

The piles of long, curved, chalky sheep skeletons took me
directly back into the story of La Huesera, Bone Woman, as
told by the gifted *cantadora* Clarissa Pinkola Estes. La Huesera lives between the worlds in a cave in the earth. As the
keeper of souls, she preserves the female lineage. La Huesera
teaches that we all begin as a bundle of bones lost somewhere in a desert, and it is our work to recover the parts.
Bone Woman waits in her cave for pilgrims to visit her and
then she helps them know what they need to know.

Here is what La Huesera said to me as we sat together in
her cave of white bones, blue sky ceiling above us, and Ireland's astonishing green blossoming all around us.

"You have been collecting the bones of your mother in
Africa, in Asia, in Russia, in Europe, and in America. And
now, here in Ireland, her bones are mended back together.
You must get on with your life separate from your mother's
bones, from her unlived dreams. Every life has unlived dreams.
Now go, live your own life." Bone Woman's message was clear
and emphatic. I heard it deeply and felt it with all my being.

Shamans speak about shape shifting, those moments in a
life when something so important changes or completes itself

that we are indeed a different shape. As I made my way back through those glorious green Irish fields I felt singular, separate from my mother for the first time.

Joining my Helix Sisters back at our country inn where we sat by the peat fire, I shared the story of La Huesera and her mandate for me to move on with my life. These dear women, who were a unique combination of both sister and mother to me, who had listened to my story for so many years, knew that this was a turning point for me. They knew that my pilgrimage had turned me upside down and this time, surrounded by their love, I had landed on my feet.

I had several more days in Ireland after my shape shifting experience. I didn't fully understand what had happened to me but I felt happy and free. More than anything I felt awed by the way the great mystery moves among our earthly existence. I realized that some inexplicable force is running through each of our lives, weaving our stories in a way that is so divinely unexpected as to take our breath away.

I certainly couldn't have planned for my encounter with Bone Woman nor found her in therapy or a book. But there she was waiting for me in the territory of the unknown, in the vast expanse of my imagination. During the final days of my pilgrimage I came to believe that both the most unexpected and the deepest healing take place in the realm of the imagination. In this multidimensional intangible space there is no need to rush or force our journey. There is no need to worry that our stories will finally come together into a whole cloth. That weaving, no matter how lopsided or strange the pattern might seem, is already being shaped by the loom of our creativity. For some the threads are pulled together through music or painting, poetry or writing, dance or drama.

It was the sacred feminine herself who had invited me to leave behind my linear known plans and to jump empty-handed into her crooked unknown. There she presented me with the most surprising revelations. To be showered by her generosity I simply needed to stay awake and alert to her signs, which were all around me. All I needed was to open the door of my imagination where I could see with child's eyes, listen with big ears, and feel with a full heart. All I needed was to return to the door that Mom had opened for me so many years ago. And so it was that I let go of my mother in the realm of the imagination, the place where she was her most authentic self and where I most cherished her.

Honoring Maud

Arrange whatever pieces come your way.
—Virginia Woolf

It would take me time to understand the far-reaching wisdom of La Huesera. Returning home I could see that my pilgrimage had been like praying a long rosary in honor of mothers. The beads of that rosary were made up of my Helix Sisters with their mothering role; Mother Mary in the Cashel Mountains and Grandma Walsh in Josie's kitchen; the cosmic mother La Huesera waiting for me in her cave of bones; and finally my encounter with Mom, saying goodbye to her in a new way. I knew there was one more mother I needed to honor in order to complete this pilgrimage.

Soon after returning from Ireland, I made the final leg of my voyage, driving east on the Mass Pike to Cambridge and right into Harvard Square. I was ten minutes away from the house of Maud Morgan, my spiritual mother. Though I didn't consciously set out to find someone like Maud, if I could have put in a request to the universe for a wise crone who could fulfill my fantasy of Mom if she had lived longer and returned to her life as an artist, surely the universe would have sent no other than Maud Morgan. Throughout my journey of rediscovering my mother and reclaiming my feminine wisdom, I was blessed to have Maud as my friend.

Arriving in bumper-to-bumper traffic in the Square, I had time to relish some of my memories from our fifteen-year friendship. Maud had told me much of her life story and I knew that as a young artist, living abroad, she had formed friendships with James Joyce and Ernest Hemingway. When she was seventy-seven, she took a six-month trip through Africa—by herself. In the 1980s during the height of the Cold War she chose to close her painting studio for a time and become a passionate antinuclear activist. Now in her mid-nineties, she was mentoring young women painters and setting up a fund in her name to support the work of aspiring artists. At ninety-two she had written her memoir, *Maud's Journey: A Life from Art.*

During our myriad of visits, Maud had talked to me a lot about the challenges of following her calling as an artist. For years she felt ill at ease with her family and battled feelings of inadequacy. For a while she even stopped painting, and only after a painful divorce was she able to start a new life and return to her art. She had taught me that the process of staying true to oneself is messy and uneven. Once she said to me, "Gail, life has lots of seasons. Just remember there will be winters and autumns surrounding the springs and summers." Maud's return to her purpose came when she was in her mid-fifties, at the same stage of life my mother was when she died.

Flooded with memories, I arrived at Maud's quiet house just outside Harvard Square. How apt, I thought, that this is the final leg of my pilgrimage, because Maud's home always feels like the house of the Great Mother to me. As was my custom, I arrived with a bouquet of flowers, this time fiery orange tulips with dark purple centers. After Maud arranged them, we sat together and had tea. As during other visits, soon I lost myself in her extraordinary face. Nine decades of joys and sorrows wound their way through a vast array of wrinkles and lines, telling so many stories I could get dizzy looking at her. Her head was surrounded by a great shock of white hair. "I want to look like Albert Einstein," she once said.

We talked and talked for hours about politics, marriage, women's empowerment, art, music, film, and spirituality. Throughout the years of our friendship I had asked her advice on everything from my power struggles with David, to how best to support difficult students, to staying brutally honest in the writing process. So rich were these conversations with Maud that I felt in some small way they made up for the talks I never had with my mother. I didn't tell Maud this, but I think, like any good spiritual mother, she knew exactly what she was doing by reflecting me so deeply.

Today, she wanted to know all about my pilgrimage to Ireland. I eagerly explained my encounter with La Huesera in the cave of white bones. "La Huesera told me to get on with my life, separate from my mother's bones and from her unlived dreams. She told me to go live my own life." Maud listened silently, intently. With her untamed white hair and long lean frame wrapped in a silver African robe, she appeared very much as I imagined Bone Woman herself might look. "I am still trying to figure out exactly what all this means," I continued, knowing that she would offer me her reflection.

Maud looked at me tenderly. "Gail, a motherless daughter has to mother to feel mothered. Since you have chosen not to have children you must find a way to mother in your work. I think you are already a spiritual mother to many of your students. Now you must do this even more consciously. Separating from your mother, I imagine you are going to enter a whole new phase of your teaching." As always, I took her counsel very seriously. Though it would be almost two years before I launched the new phase of my work, who else but Maud could have initiated this next chapter of my life as a spiritual mother.

I drove back to my mountain home resplendent with the full bloom of summer and I, too, was bursting with ideas. A week after I returned, Maud sent me one of her small collages depicting a primordial fish swimming in avocado green water. Scrawled on the back, she described the welfare of the recent bouquet I had brought to her, "I found another vase! The tulips are spreading out, surrounding me and making me happy, Love, Maud." Glued on the last page of my Ireland journal, Maud's card represents the final blessing of my pilgrimage, the final bead in the long rosary honoring my mothers.

Now my psyche knew that I had completed a cycle in my life and I was awaiting confirmation of the next one. Several months after my pilgrimage I had this dream: *I am an infant in the woods drinking the milk from a young goat. Slowly I grow up and the goat grows up. Then the goat turns into a beautiful unicorn and I ride on her back through the woods.*

The dream resonated on many levels. At my birth when I was allergic to my mother's milk, it was goat's milk that kept me alive. I was born in January, growing up in the sign of the Capricorn goat. In Jungian literature, the unicorn represents a woman's deep feminine center, her spiritual core.

Riding on the unicorn affirmed Maud's mandate, my readiness to make conscious my role as a spiritual mother. I began work in earnest on the designing of a year-long program I decided to call "Grace Spiritual Growth Training," which would integrate spiritual development with social responsibility. I called it "Grace" because I was fond of the formal definition of grace as an unmerited gift from God. I kept Maud abreast of my progress. After about six months I called to ask if I could pay a visit to share the brochure design with her. "Yes, of course," she said in her gravelly voice. "But hurry up and get here before I die." I had always loved her wry humor, but I knew that she had taken a bad fall on the ice and her health was failing quickly.

What I didn't know was that this would be my final visit with my ninety-six-year-old friend. This time I arrived with two dozen royal purple and canary yellow irises. We had our tea and briefly discussed my Grace brochure. I could see her energy was limited and I wanted to hear more about her life, as if I were unconsciously making up for the wasted moments that still haunted me from my last visit with my own mother. Though clearly her physical strength was declining, Maud's mind was as sharp as ever and her humor in rare form. "I am not dead yet, so I thought I would have another show," she said to me. She was working on a new series of collages. She could cut out the pieces of the collage, but her hands trembled too much to glue them in place. She'd recently hired a young woman artist to serve as her apprentice. How I hoped this young woman knew how extraordinarily blessed she was to fill that role.

Maud's bedroom was in an A-frame structure with abundant sun pouring through skylights in the ceiling. She set up her "studio" beside her bed, and this is where we sat together. Maud said to me, "I've learned to be very careful with my precious energy, using it only for what I really love. Sometimes I sleep twelve hours at a stretch, and then go right to my work table. There is less difference," she explained, "between my dream and waking life. These two worlds are becoming seamless."

I watched Maud move her brightly colored shapes into a design as she explained, "I don't know exactly what will emerge, I just trust that the pieces will fall into place. Virginia Woolf once said, 'Arrange whatever pieces come your way.'

That's what I've tried to do with my life, Gail." As she worked and talked I wanted to stay in her presence forever, taking in her wisdom and her wit, being filled with her unbridled imagination and her openhearted relationship with her death. How blessed and happy I felt to be nourished by Maud.

Maud died at home a few months later. The day I heard about her death I read passages from her memoir to bring her spirit close to me. I especially loved this paragraph toward the end. "Now I end this story of a life like any other, both fragile and tough; the fragility evident from the start, the toughness formed en route. I'm kinder to myself now, less critical of the good and bad things that occur in the present or past. Maybe later I will start to worry about death and dying, but I haven't quite finished living enough yet to forfeit my spare time to apprehension. As Isak Dinesen said of herself, 'I am a messenger who has been sent on a long journey to declare that there is hope in the world.'"

The next time I was in Boston I went to the Museum of Fine Arts, which houses some of her paintings. I sat in front of one of Maud's famous self-portraits depicting her Einsteinian white hair curling out from under a great floppy white hat. Indeed her enigmatic presence filled me with enormous hope. I thanked her for being my spiritual mother, for allowing me to at least imagine the kind of life my mother might have created if she'd made other choices, if she hadn't been so sick and had lived longer, or perhaps if fate had landed her in a different city. Saying goodbye to Maud I realized that so many people in our lives mother us, and that this unequivocally precious process goes on for such a long time. Now it was my turn to mother.

PART FOUR

In the House of the Great Mother

Passing My Wisdom to Others

O Wisdom Goddess!
Your essence alone is present
within every life, every event.
Your living power flows freely as this universe.
You are expressed fully, even by the smallest
    movement.
Wherever I go, and wherever I look,
I perceive only you my blissful Mother,
radiating as pure cosmic play,
Earth, water, fire, air, space and consciousness,
are simply your projected forms.
There is nothing else.

—*Hymn of Ramprasad to Kali*
(translated by Lex Hixon)

Becoming a Spiritual Mother

Protecting the Lineage of the Feminine

Evening Star who gathers everything
Shining dawn scattered
You bring the sheep and the goats,
You bring the child back to its mother.
—Sappho (translated by Diane Rayor)

About a year after Maud's death I launched my work as spiritual mother. Around the same time I started my menopause. How perfectly upside down that I formally began my mothering in the phase of womanhood when normal childbearing is finished. I was entering what my friend Chris Northrup calls menopausal wisdom. It is a period, she says, when our brains are literally rewired, liberating us to pursue emotional and spiritual growth. Surely it was an auspicious time for me to become a spiritual mother, surely a fertile time to pay tribute to the sacred feminine, who honors emotional intelligence and the interior life, who bows to the irrational and the paradoxical as guardians of the mystical, and who holds the values of inclusiveness and collaboration as the highest form of worship. It

was my time to join the ancient lineage of spiritual mothers
—mentors, teachers, healers, therapists, and grandmothers—
who protect and pass on the wisdom of the feminine.

As it turned out this was also an auspicious time in our
culture to become a spiritual mother and offer my Grace Spiritual Growth Training program. Many people were either leaving their faith traditions or in need of something additional.
The betrayal of the sacred feminine in most major spiritual
traditions had left people hungry for the nondogmatic and all-
inclusive nourishment of the feminine. People had become
fed up with religious hierarchies that strangled the imagination and spirit of the seeker.

As I designed Grace, I realized that the fundamental principles of spiritual mothering nourished not just the individual,
but offered the very practices that we need for a more peaceful and sustainable planet. Protecting the inner life against
all odds in a world dominated by outer masculine values of
thought, speed, action, and achievement was something I had
learned the hard way. Now I wanted to help my students bring
this critical balance of inner and outer into their lives. Working with women globally, I had seen that the conscious feminine did much of her healing through radical presence and
nondoing, offering an antidote to our addiction to fixing
and consuming on both the emotional and ecological levels.
And most important for me, the practice of spiritual mothering cultivated an appreciation of complexity and respect for diversity on all levels—personal, political, and spiritual. Clearly,
protecting the lineage of the feminine was as much a social
mandate as a spiritual one.

With all this in mind I created Grace as a program of engaged spirituality combining rigorous personal inquiry, service
to the world, ecological mindfulness, and prayer and meditation. By now I have offered the Grace training for fifteen years

to hundreds of men and women from around the world. Grace Spiritual Growth Training is essentially a place where I help people protect their interior lives and create spiritual family. Yes, how perfectly ironic for a woman who lost her own family and chose not to have children. How deliciously ironic that the lapsed daughter of a devout Catholic mother was now shepherding her own charges back to the sacred. Finally separate from my mother, I could go about the kind of mothering that fulfilled my own dreams. I could go about my work with my feminine intact, with all the stories from women all over the world informing the way I would practice spiritual mothering. Coming full circle, I became a mother to those orphaned values that Mom had abandoned so long ago.

My work as a spiritual mother is still essentially about stories. In my small meditation room looking out over the Ashokan Reservoir, two pairs of prayer beads sit next to each other. My mother's black rosary beads are so worn from her prayers and mine that they are now more the color of pale wood than black. Her story and mine are woven into these beads and I imagine our Hail Marys are one voice now.

The second pair contains hundreds of brightly colored beads, each one different. They are made of glass, stone, shell, silver, and brass, and they take the form of birds, turtles, bears, Buddhas, crosses, and ancient goddesses. The stories in these beads contain my work as a spiritual mother, for each one was given to me by one of my students as he or she created a personal strand of prayer beads. These stories are from people of every imaginable walk of life, in their twenties and thirties as well as their sixties and seventies. They are from African Americans, Asians, Latinas, Indians, Europeans, and Russians coming together as Jews, Muslims, Catholics, Lutherans, Baptists, Buddhists, Hindus, and atheists. The young girl from Wilmington, whose status as an outsider birthed her love of diversity, has grown up. Finally, I see so clearly how a place inside you that hurts can turn into a passion that heals.

On most mornings after a silent meditation during which David and I sit side by side, I pray with both of these strings of beads. My mother's spiritual path was contained by one tradition, and mine has become a blend of the world's traditions. Inexorably my mother, myself as her daughter, and myself as a spiritual mother come together in these prayers.

Many of the stories contained in my string of prayer beads involve people encountering joy and suffering, hope and despair, or good and evil as they make their way through life. A good spiritual mother knows how to guide a person into the strong heat of these great unfixables, and in this fiery process she initiates a person into spiritual maturity. Like Demeter, the goddess of the hearth, a spiritual mother keeps a person close to the heat and passion of existence, away from the cold meaninglessness of an overly affluent or lazy modern life. Like all mothers, a spiritual mother must find the delicate balance between protecting and reassuring, and then letting go and nurturing freedom. It was a balance my own mother had taught so well.

My unfolding as a spiritual mother offered me yet another window into Mom as well as a more intimate view of the universal feminine. I could feel the primal roots of the feminine—receiving, nourishing, and giving birth—at work inside me as I created a safe space for my students, loved and nurtured them, and eventually as they grew into spiritual maturity, sent them on their way. I could follow those primal roots inside my mother as she made our Brecks Lane home a sanctuary, fed my imagination and voracious love of life, and then let me go even as she was close to death. Now I could see how vibrantly and heartbreakingly creative the process of mothering was. I could understand how much joy and pain this had brought my mother.

Like all mothering, mine has matured over time. As a young spiritual mother I wanted to fix my students and take away their pain. I know now that my desire to fix came from my fear of their suffering—from depression or divorce, AIDS or cancer, or the death of a loved one. If the suffering didn't come from one of those demons, then it might have stemmed from despair at the loss of a job or work that strangled the soul, the discovery of a husband who had cheated for many years, or a suicidal teenage child. The terrible desire to fix is the same shadow mother who overprotects or smothers a child. Only after many years of guiding people can I now say with utter conviction that I believe that people want the truth more than they want to avoid suffering. Each time I encourage a student to go fearlessly into the fires of his or her pain, I know that in the unbearable heat transformation will occur. I know that there, at the center of the blaze, the seeker will meet the Great Mother as she administers her ancient alchemy.

Over time, I learned to resist both the impulse to fix and the desperate, and often unconscious, request that I somehow make life simple. This is a plea that comes from almost all my students. Couldn't my work be just rewarding instead of also monotonous? Why do the people I love the most always bring me the most pain? How could there be a benevolent God if my thirty-year-old son has just died of AIDS? Where can I ever find hope in a world full of genocide, war, and terrorism? How I wished that I could take away the dual nature of our human predicament, offering a clean resolution to its inexplicable complexity. It was here that my appreciation for the sacred feminine was especially heightened. Through her refusal to take simplistic either/or positions, and with her firm insistence that we hold all the awful messiness of paradox, she gave me the central requirement for helping people grow up spiritually.

As I wrestled with these issues I frequently mused about how Mom came to grips with these questions. How often did she waver about when to be tough or soft with me? Did she struggle to explain the terrible beauty of life to me? Perhaps she knew that eventually I might see that her own life was the answer to that paradox. Like me, did she finally come to accept that there is no "expert" way to love? We can only hope to give our best, and that will surely be imperfect. Before she died just a few years younger than I am now, did she come to believe that this fragile imperfection is love itself?

And so, back in my meditation room I tenderly hold the string of colorful prayer beads representing my students' stories. It is held together by my fragile imperfection, each story reflecting a face of the feminine or another blessing from my mother.

When the Heart Cradles
the Irrational

Love of God is pure when joy and suffering inspire
an equal degree of gratitude.

—Simone Weil

Imagine a beautiful woman, her skin the color of dark honey,
her eyes deep as an ancient holy well drawing you down.
Azar is telling her story to my group of Grace students at the
monastery in the Hudson Valley where we gather several times
a year for our retreats.

"I grew up in Egypt. My father was a devout Muslim and
a leader in our community, and my mother was a healer. I
adored Egypt and my childhood was a happy one. In my twenties I moved to America where I married, had a daughter, and
became a successful businesswoman and a role model for other
Muslim women in my community. My life was going well.
One night, I was on my way to my car after work and I was
brutally raped in the parking lot. In that same year I would

lose my job and learn that my husband had been unfaithful for many years. My whole life fell apart. Depression and despair were followed by suicidal feelings. During this time I found Gail's book *The Rhythm of Compassion* and this is how I come to be standing before you in this Benedictine monastery. I am a long, long way from that happy young girl in Egypt. I don't know if I will ever feel hope again."

As we listen to Azar's story, light streams through the tall windows of the monastery overlooking the mighty Hudson River. I feel only this strong light can hold her sorrow.

"Dear, dear Azar, how brave you were to gather yourself and come to the monastery and how brave you are to tell us your story. Thank you so very much," I begin.

"No one can take away your despair. You must feel it until it runs its course. No one can go through the dark night of the soul for you. You must do that yourself. But you can surround yourself with those who love you and ask them to pray for you with all their strength. Don't forget the natural world is waiting to generously offer you its incomparable solace. You can get professional help and if you choose you can find the right medication until your depression lifts. And it helps to surround yourself with music and poetry that lift you up. Given your tradition, Rumi and Hafiz wouldn't be bad companions. Remember the Hafiz poem that we studied at our last retreat?

"Wayfarer,

Your whole mind and body have been tied
To the foot of the Divine Elephant
With a thousand golden chains.

Now, begin to rain intelligence and compassion
Upon all your tender, wounded cells

And realize the profound absurdity
Of thinking

That you can ever go Anywhere
Or do Anything

Without God's will.

"And as soon as you are ready, go back out into the world and help the young Muslim women in your community. There is no stronger medicine than service.

"Now, close your eyes. When you are quiet inside, simply allow the first image you associate with hope to come to you." In most interactions with my students, I am inviting them to cultivate a radical trust in their intuition.

Azar closes her eyes. "Almost immediately I saw my father at morning prayers and I was filled with peace. He says I must be strong and I will get through this. Whenever I pray he is at my side."

Now Azar is weeping. Her father's presence is filling the room along with the light pouring in through the tall stately windows, reminding us that the dark night of the soul is a sure stepping-stone on the path to mature faith. And that path is certain to be lined with both light and dark for those who are brave enough to travel there.

After the retreat Azar returned home and for some time she felt her strength slowly being restored. Then I received this e-mail.

Dearest Gail,

After Grace I had a wonderful month when things were going smoothly. For now the medication is helping my depression. But still I am feeling disconnected again. Disconnected from myself and I guess mostly from God. I am not meditating or praying either. I feel like I take one step forward and then two backwards. I am so tired of feeling like a spiritual yo-yo; close to God then far away again, meditating regularly then not at all. Feeling hope for the world and then complete despair. Sometimes I wish I didn't feel things so deeply. I ask myself, why can't I just get myself together?

I feel ashamed telling you this, Gail, like I am not doing a good job as your student. I want you to give me the answers; it's so hard to take responsibility for my own life. Silly me, I don't even know what I am really asking you. For courage I think.

With love and respect, Azar

Dear One Azar,

Thank you so much for your brave and honest letter. I am so glad the medication is helping your depression. Dear Azar, like all of us you are much too hard on yourself. None of us would ever be so tough on others as we are on ourselves. It's true, isn't it? Please give yourself a break, be gentle and kind with yourself. You have been through so much and healing takes time.

Like any partnership, our relationship with the divine is not always going to be smooth or comfortable. So often it's by riding through the rough times that we deepen our faith. Even when we fall off during the ride we are still plunging further into understanding.

And it's very important to remember that the actual rhythm of the spiritual journey is to feel connected at certain times and then disconnected. The tension of feeling close to God and then far away is the very thing that helps us find a mature relationship with our creator. Said another way, respecting this tension creates a strong foundation for mature faith. And as you have heard me say many times, it's when we go toward the tension of any opposite, neither pushing away what we don't like nor clinging to the part we do like, that's when we grow strong inside. What if you went toward your disconnection and explored it with wide-eyed curiosity. What do you find in that disconnection? How does it look, feel, smell, sound, and taste? What is the disconnection trying to teach you? I imagine you might be very surprised by what you discover.

Your feeling of taking one step forward and two steps backwards is like a spiritual cha-cha-cha. As with all dance, if we can relax and surrender to the steps, our movement is more graceful and enjoyable. Then, in our back and forth rhythm we can even find pleasure and acceptance for our human condition. I have seen you moving across the monastery floor at our Saturday night celebrations and I know you are a good dancer, my dear Azar!

In closing, I remind you to work with the Metta Loving Kindness prayer that we have turned to so often during our retreats. Just say it whenever you start to feel disconnected. You might be in your car, at work, eating a meal, or before you sleep at night. I would like to end with Metta for you.

Azar,
May you be filled with loving kindness,
May you be well,
May you be peaceful and at ease,
May you be happy.

With love and blessings, Gail

I decided to keep some of my correspondence with my students in the old wooden JWS box that holds certain of Mom's treasured letters to me. I like to imagine that when my mother's letters touch the words that I sent to Azar, perhaps Mom can feel my mothering next to hers. Perhaps she, too, is blessing Azar. As the next years unfolded, what would my mother have told Azar when she stayed in a destructive marriage far too long, or when she battled her depression like a brave warrior in a fight for her very life? No matter how many retreats she attended, how much we all prayed for her, or how much counsel I gave, Azar's life fell apart again and again.

As for me, I often grew impatient with my spiritual daughter. I couldn't understand why she stayed in a life that was dead. I couldn't fathom what kept her from moving on. Mercifully, when my impatience had reached new heights, I remembered my own excruciatingly slow process of healing. I wondered what would have happened if those who loved me had given up during the long years of my denial when my heart was banged shut against the truth of my life. My compassion returned like a bolt of lightning thrown down by the hand of the Goddess, and I felt her stern reprimand at my core: "The greatest trap for any teacher is arrogance." With that slap of lightning came the Great Mother's unmistakable reminder that we are all together in this small boat on the great sea of life.

Some years have passed and Azar is back at our monastery on the Hudson River. She is part of a group of students who have been with me for five and six years. They know one another well and are mature as a community. Finally, Azar is taking legal action to leave her marriage. Finally, she has had enough. She is asking for our Grace community's prayers to help keep her strong in the upcoming days when she will leave her husband and start a new life. Given Azar's cultural background this is especially brave. All of us empathize as she struggles mightily with the idea that she still loves the man who has caused her so much pain. Her sharp intellect tries to make rational sense out of the fact that she must leave what she loves.

I remind her that there is no way to understand the situation rationally. "Go to your heart, the place that cradles the irrational. Now let your heart guide you to honor all your contrasting feelings: your lingering desire to stay in your marriage and your desperate need to leave; your sadness about ending this cycle, and your joy about beginning a new life. Hold the beautiful mess of both. It's the only way to be true to yourself."

Supporting Azar, I wanted to bow deeply to the sacred feminine. I wanted to apologize for all the years that I had betrayed Her holy wisdom—her warm embrace of all that "doesn't make sense" but is nonetheless true. I thought of all the times that my students had tried to wrap their brains around the inexplicable, only to end up in more pain. I thought of all those deaths, divorces, depressions, and crises of faith when I wondered what to say to offer comfort. Then the Great Mother would come to my rescue, reminding me that the realm of the unreasonable is the very heartbeat of existence, that to be alive we must feel as well as think. Sadly, too, the Great Mother reminded me that part of my own mother's heartbreak was my betrayal of her irrational and emotional brilliance. Again I thought of my diehard allegiance to the rational and the explainable at my father's dinner table, and again I searched for self-forgiveness.

"Dear one Azar, you know that our prayers are with you. You know that one of your most trusted sacred places is the natural world and you will go there to gain comfort and clarity. There is something else you need to do as you end your marriage. Close your eyes and ask for guidance."

Quieting herself and listening for the pulse beat of her intuition Azar is so lovely, simultaneously fierce and fragile. "I must go to my father's grave. I must ask for his blessing. This will give me strength." As tears pour out of her eyes, I remember her father's presence from years ago in this very same room. Azar's father's steadfast invisible presence shows us once again that love never dies. Later, as she is leaving, I give Azar a hug and tell her that I love her. She thanks me for staying with her for all these years.

Then, as is my custom at the end of each retreat, I went outside to a wooden bench on the cloister walk and offered prayers of gratitude. Over the years I have spent many hours of prayer and walking meditation on this sheltered brick walkway, and it is my favorite spot in the monastery. The cloister walk offers expansive views of the Hudson River and sitting there I remembered that the Algonquian name for the Hudson was Muhheakantuck, "river that flows two ways." The deep, ancient waterway held the truth of so much of my teaching, even in its very name. Watching the river and thinking about Azar and her father, once again that mysterious feeling of oneness descended on me, the certain knowing that when our stories weave in and out of each other, they change us and become part of us. I saw that like Azar's father, my mother's invisible presence had never left me. And like me with Azar, Mom had patiently stayed with me for a long time before I did what was necessary in my life. None of this made rational sense, but in my heart I could cradle it all.

Honoring the Great Mother
by Embracing the Other

You all know, I think, what I am trying to say—
that we must try not to end up with stereotypes of
those we oppose, even as they slip all of us into
their stereotypes. And who are we? Let us not do
to ourselves as those others do to us: try to put ourselves into one all-inclusive category—the vir-
tuous ones as against the evil ones, or the decent
ones as against the malicious, prejudiced ones, or
the well educated as against the ignorant.
                                        —Dr. Martin Luther King

The custom at my Grace retreats is to reserve the final evening
for celebration. Abiding by my mother's dictum that every
woman must know how to throw a great party, these evenings
are occasions for dancing, ecstatic prayer, and wearing wild
costumes. Over the years we have dressed as our shadow, our
most secret selves, and our perfectionism gone astray. It's a

marvelous site to see a costumed Mother Superior coyly open her black habit transforming herself into a burlesque performer in hot pink silk and feathers. A special marvel when the transformation takes place in a monastery dining room turned into a dance floor.

For these celebrations I often invite an artist to lead us in the song and dance of his or her tradition. One evening a gifted Jewish singer, the granddaughter of a famous rabbi, came to join us. Ronit visited us during a time when things had heated up in the Middle East and the fragile dreams of peace had been shattered once again. She spoke passionately of her own dreams for peace. Ronit honored her grandfather by teaching us glorious Israeli songs that we sang in Hebrew while spinning wildly and kicking up our feet to the sound of the saxophone. I went to bed that night dreaming that Israel was a place filled with song instead of war.

The next morning we gathered for our last session. Though I had slept well, others had not. Before our opening prayer Nassrin came to me saying she was very upset and she needed some help. Dark circles under her eyes told me of her sleepless night.

"I am very upset this morning. As all of you know I am a practicing Muslim. Part of why this group is so special to me is that we come from many traditions and we honor and celebrate our differences. But last night I felt dishonored. I felt that Ronit presented the situation in the Middle East in an unfair and lopsided way, telling only the Jewish side of things. She did not include the Muslim point of view. I could not join in the song and dance. I had to leave."

The room was very quiet as Nassrin spoke. I felt terrible that I had not seen her leave and gone to comfort her. I felt like a mother who had let down her child, who had unwittingly caused her pain. Then, as if in answer to my prayers, Edward said, "Gail, I would like to respond to Nassrin."

We knew that Edward was the most devout of all the Jews in our group. He had considered rabbinical studies but decided to become an architect instead. He was greatly loved by the group and we thought of him as our philosopher king.

"Nassrin, I am really sorry last night was offensive to you. I can't change the situation in the Middle East but I was wondering if you might teach me a simple Muslim prayer and I might teach you a Jewish prayer. Maybe a prayer about our hopes for peace."

I felt such admiration for Edward; his instincts were so genuine and precise. He reminded me yet again of the miraculous nature of group process with exactly the right person offering the wisdom that was needed at a particular moment. I just needed to get out of the way, like a good mother who knows when to step aside and allow her children to empower one another.

"Yes, I would like that, Edward, I would like that a lot," Nassrin said, looking him square in the eyes, her face open and beseeching. Her face was a map of the hopes and dreams of thousands of ordinary Muslims whom we never hear about in the news, who want to find a way to get along with the Jews. "A very old and simple Muslim prayer for peace goes like this." First Nassrin recited the prayer in Arabic, the sounds of her voice taking me back to my village in Africa where I had often attended services in the sun-baked red clay mosque. The intonations of her ancient language were an elixir for my soul, a melodic antidote for the stereotype of Muslims since 9/11. Then Nassrin paused, her entire being filled with the prayer, and shifted to English.

Oh God,
You are Peace.
From You comes Peace,
To You returns Peace.

Revive us with a salutation of Peace,
And lead us to your abode of Peace.

"Now, Edward, let's say it together." The whole room resonated as her light vibrant voice blended with Edward's deep baritone. They recited the prayer several times with such gravitas that it became more than two voices; it became an entire mosque praying together.

Then Nassrin asked Edward, "Would you teach me a Jewish prayer now?" In that moment my love for Nassrin came on me with such force I couldn't hold back my tears. There she was in all her vulnerable beauty, teaching us about the complex art of standing firm while also staying open and flexible, teaching us that it was possible to remain true to one's own beliefs, yet open to the perceived "other."

"Nassrin, first thank you for teaching me your prayer, it's lovely. A passage I like very much is from the prayers we say on *shabbat*, the sabbath, and it's called 'Shalom Rav.' I'd love to share it with you and I think it's a worthy companion to your prayer. It goes like this. I will say it first in Hebrew." Edward would have been a fine rabbi, I thought as I listened to his rich and flawless Hebrew. And then switching into English, he began with a slow cadence, finding his way into the layers of meaning that reveal themselves when we have said a prayer many times.

You have given us the power, O God, to bring peace and justice into the world. May we always love peace and pursue it, and love our fellow creatures. Fill your children with kindness, wisdom, and love. Then shall they learn to live at peace.

Blessed is the Lord, Teacher of Peace.

Nassrin and Edward knelt together on the old monastery floor reciting their prayers in Arabic, Hebrew, and English.

Then they taught us the words, and our prayers joined those of the monks chanting in the chapel below, where the brothers had prayed five times a day for the past hundred years. Then I remembered fifteen years of Sunday mass sitting next to my mother as she prayed. Prayer, that invisible force weaving together the past, the present, and the future, is one of the rare vehicles that can mend our differences into a fabric of fragile hope.

Praying with my students, I was never more convinced that our chance for world peace lies with ordinary people of different faith traditions, cultures, races, and genders coming together face to face. Facing one another we become bigger than any one of us, big enough to hold both our differences and our longing for global cooperation. And our delicate hope is held in the strong arms of this synthesis of individual differences and universal longing. I am certain that these are the strong arms of the Great Mother and that the highest way we can honor her is by facing whatever "other" exists inside us or in the world around us.

But this is hard to do, isn't it? Sometimes what's most difficult is taking back a disowned aspect of our selves, our darkness or despair, our softness or emotions. At other times what's most challenging is trying to embrace a part of the world that holds very different ideas or values from us. Fortunately, one spills over into the other, and once we have reclaimed a disowned piece of ourselves we can take back that same part of the world, and vice versa. A particular Grace retreat seemed preordained to teach this advanced lesson from the curriculum of the sacred feminine.

I have left the monastery in the Hudson Valley and now I am in a small cobblestone village in the Netherlands where the monastery has been converted into a conference center. The steeple towers above the flat farmlands where Holland borders Germany. I love the sound of the bell ringing every hour.

During our days of silent meditation the church bell blends with the small Tibetan bell that I ring to signal the end of a meditation round. Two bells ringing, blending traditions.

This group of students is an international family from Holland, Germany, Belgium, Russia, Canada, and the United States. Having met for four years we are now swimming in deep waters together. Our inquiry is taking us into those territories that I most want to explore but for which I don't have any maps. This is simultaneously the most exciting and the most challenging phase of my spiritual mothering. My relationship with my students seems similar to what I imagine a relationship between parent and child might be as the child matures and becomes less dependent and more like a cherished and respected friend. This is the very stage of relationship that I missed and still longed for with my own mother.

We are discussing God. To be exact, I have asked my students what is required to have a mature relationship with their God, a relationship where we no longer deflect the responsibility for good and evil onto God. I have asked them to find the particular deal they have struck with God. To inspire their inquiry I have just shown them a PBS documentary titled *Faith and Doubt at Ground Zero*, a stirring account of people's spiritual inquiry after 9/11, including graphic images of people jumping hand in hand from the Twin Towers. We are all visibly shaken after the film.

I see that Rene's handsome face is especially troubled. A successful writer, Rene has a wonderful wife who is a medical doctor and three sons who are archetypes of Dutch loveliness, with platinum blond hair, blue eyes, and rosy cheeks.

"When I think of God I feel nothing. Absolutely nothing. I fear there is nothing. It's all a big joke. I feel despair. What if there really is nothing, just destruction, like the Hell we've just seen." Rene begins to sob, deep racking sobs.

"Dear Rene, you are on your way to a mature relationship with your God," I say, to his surprise. Over time I had learned that real sacred ground covered a territory far more vast than the mind could comprehend, but the heart could usually find an opening into its spacious expanse. This holy ground was made fertile by the nutrients of the unknown and the inexplicable, enriched by whatever most frightened us or was most unexpected. This was the garden that the Great Mother tended.

"Would you trust me if I told you this existential nothingness you are feeling is a doorway to God? Would you be willing to open this door and see what you find?"

I can tell by the deep furrows in his brow that Rene doesn't like what I have asked him. But he has seen me guide people so often into the fires of their greatest fear that we are now held in that field of trust. In that moment I am so aware of how trust must be built over time, and how it requires just the right amount of gentle waiting and firm pushing forward. Indeed, it requires the feminine and the masculine working in harmony. I know this is a time to urge him forward and I am relieved when he says, "Yes, I feel I have no other choice."

"Good for you. Close your eyes, quiet yourself, and trust your imagination to guide you. Visualize the door to your nothingness and when you are ready, go through the door." I know that traveling into the unknown he could have no more worthy companion than his supple imagination.

"The door is giant and black. There is no doorknob and I have to hurl myself against it to open it. When I open the door it's just black, vast all-consuming blackness. Now I see fire, death, and suffering. Just total destruction, just like the rubble at Ground Zero," Rene says.

"Now I am going to ask you to do something difficult. I want you to bring your three sons in front of you. I want you to imagine them in front of you in the middle of this Hell."

As I say this to the handsome father standing before me, I pray that I haven't gone too far. I remember that I can't do this by myself and I silently ask for Mother Mary's help. I am reminded that growing up spiritually has little to do with comfort and that from fearlessness freedom is born. Rene is doubled over in pain now and we are all crying, feeling like we, too, are standing with his sons at Ground Zero.

"Dear Rene, your sons have something to say to you. Listen well."

"They are handing me a small delicate flower. Please care for this, Papa, they say. You must care for it. My boys have taken my hand and they are showing me other small flowers growing out of the cracks of the horrible destruction."

We are all speechless with gratitude toward Rene's willingness to enter his existential despair. For many of us, confronting despair is one of the scariest "others" inside both ourselves and in the world. During our retreats we have often spoken about the paradoxical necessity of going toward despair in order to find hope. Each of us knows this intellectually but we also know the enormous courage it takes to actually feel the depth of our hopelessness. The head part is so easy and the heart part is so hard. But only then, when we have worked the Goddess's messy fertile ground with our deepest hidden feelings, can we plant the seeds of mature sustainable hope.

Later that afternoon Rene wrote a small affirmation and we put it to music. "I choose to water the small flower of hope in my cosmos," we sang in English, then in Dutch, German, French, and Russian. The sweet simple melody transported us all into the realm of hope, that place at once so delicate and so fierce.

That night I went to bed exhausted and full of gratitude for my work. With Rene's song in my head, I fell asleep musing about how taking sides with just one end of any paradox will eventually force us to face its opposite. As often occurred during our retreats, I had a dream that reflected the day's teaching. And as I would soon discover, it also proved prescient for what was about to unfold.

> I am teaching in a room divided by a sliding screen. One side says "good" and the other side says "evil." I try to teach on each separate side of the screen. I feel split in half and it's impossible to make contact with people. I insist on getting rid of the screen so I can teach with good and evil together. I feel much better.

The next morning we gathered again to share dreams and continue our discussions. Like me, many of my students experience important dreams during our retreats and today Michaela says she wants to share. Michaela is one of the introverts in this group and when she speaks to us in her quiet way it's always precious.

"Last night I had the same dream that I have had for many years. I am sure our discussion about hope and despair has brought this dream again. I dream that I am a wild horse, free and beautiful, riding the currents of life. I am the life force itself creating life. Then, I come to a crossroads in the woods and I turn into a giant snake. I begin to eat everything in my wake. I am the destroyer of life. I can't bear it. I don't want to destroy, I only want to give life." Michaela is weeping, her face revealing that special kind of naked beauty that comes when a person shows his or her pain.

"Dear one Michaela, take your time, and when you are ready speak to the snake. What does she say to you?"

Michaela paused and gathered herself. Then she closed her eyes and looked within for her answer. And we, too, closed our eyes waiting for our snake to speak.

"The snake says that giving and taking life is one large circle. Creation and destruction are two parts of a larger whole.

She says that I must no longer run away from the destructive parts of myself."

At that moment I felt such tenderness toward my charge. In our retreats we had spent considerable time working to befriend whatever we had made into "the other"—both inside ourselves as well as in the external world. As part of the Grace program, my students were involved in some form of service that brought them in touch with an aspect of society that they might otherwise push away. We were trying to learn that what we push away in the world, we also push away inside ourselves, and vice versa. I knew that Michaela stayed away from the destructive forces in the world and that this revelation could be key to her interior development as well as her leadership role in society.

"Michaela, I am so proud of you. You have been working on this issue for all the years I've known you. Now you are ready to integrate these parts of yourself. Let's go back to Thich Nhat Hanh's poem "Please Call Me By My True Names," where he shows us that we are all both creator and destroyer of life." The Zen master's poems and his life story were central to my teaching the concept of befriending the other. As a Vietnamese monk, he had witnessed the brutal death of many of his countrymen at the hands of the Americans. Yet it was he who chaired the Vietnamese Buddhist peace delegation during the war and for many years worked closely with some of the very Vietnam vets who had killed his people.

> I am a frog swimming happily
> In the clear water of a pond.
> And I am the grass-snake
> That silently feeds itself on the frog.

> I am the child in Uganda, all skin and bones,
> my legs as thin as bamboo sticks.

And I am the arms merchant,
Selling deadly weapons to Uganda.

I am the twelve-year-old girl,
refugee on a small boat,
who throws herself into the ocean
after being raped by a sea pirate.
And I am the pirate,
My heart not yet capable
Of seeing and loving.

"The poem's genius is in how clearly and simply it reminds us that we have right inside us the aspects that we most reject in the world. Our challenge is to bring those 'other' parts into our hearts and learn compassion for them. If we can do that, then we're free."

"Of course, I love that poem," Michaela says gently, pausing to take in Thich Nhat Hanh's elegant teaching. "I know these things intellectually with my mind but it's so much harder to apply them to myself, to my feelings. It's difficult for me to admit that I am both the wild horse and the giant snake; that I give and I take life." Again she is quiet, wrestling with the enormity of embracing the dark side of her human nature.

In the silence I feel the presence of the divine mother revealing the sequence of the evolving feminine. "Yes, first you must feel and then you must embrace the irrational. But far more challenging is my invitation to take back whatever part of you and the world that you have most separated from. In the highest celebration of the feminine there is no separation. Everything is connected. This is the hard part." I can feel the divine mother grin impishly at me and I realize that later I will have to really think about this. Back to Michaela. "What happens to you when you push away the giant snake part of your nature, dear one?"

After a long pregnant pause in which each one of us in the room confronts his or her own dark side, we hear her say, "I see how much energy I waste holding on to the wild horse and pushing away the giant snake. It feels like I am trying to hold back a powerful dam and I am exhausted, I want to let go. I want to admit that I have both impulses inside me, like all of life. What a big relief it is to just acknowledge that I create and I destroy."

I nod, knowing that feeling of relief. "Can you see that this reconciliation of opposites is what allows for the full blossoming of your spiritual maturity? When we integrate the other, when there are fewer and fewer things that we separate from within ourselves and in the world, we enter the unitive state, the state of mature love. We could say that in this realm that embraces all, we find ourselves cheek to cheek with God."

"Yes, yes," Michaela agreed eagerly. "My wild horse and giant snake are a lot like Rene's small flower of hope in the middle of destruction. I see you can't have one without the other. I see that a real relationship with the sacred is not some simplistic notion where God makes everything easy and the world is just good. A true relationship is paradoxical and juicy and demanding. And this is much more exciting!" Michaela's face is luminous, she is on fire with her revelation. Now that she has integrated creation and destruction within herself, her concept of God can include both those parts and she will be more able to deal with those dualistic forces in the world. At that moment I thought of Thomas Merton's statement that I love so much, "Our idea about God says much more about us than it does about God."

Witnessing Michaela it came on me clearly that I was grateful for the opposites between me and my mother. She had wanted to belong to a conservative established society and I had created my life within an alternative culture; she had children but gave up her artistic talent and I had my work but gave up having a family; she found deep faith within a traditional dogma and I found abiding comfort in an eclectic spiritual worldview. I would never have become the person I was without the tension of our opposites. Then I thought about all the mothers and daughters who I knew and I rejoiced at the seeming opposites between them, for I knew that this tension was the Great Mother at work.

That afternoon was reserved for a silent walking retreat with the landscape as teacher. As they hiked the serene pastoral farmlands and forests surrounding the old monastery, I asked my students to contemplate how the earth informs us about embracing opposites. Backpacks full of picnics, favorite poetry, journals and drawing materials, we all set out knowing that there was no more eloquent teacher of the duality than the Earth herself. Having spent many hours walking this land I felt a deep kinship with certain places. Soon I stopped near a favorite tumbling stream on the edge of a large clover pasture full of cows. The field sat just near the border of Holland and Germany.

All around me the Goddess's handiwork is apparent; light and shadow, birth and death, rock and water, all exist side by side. Musing about Michaela's beautiful work that morning brought me back to my own dream about the room with the sliding screen separating good and evil. Then I remembered the feeling of the divine mother's impish grin as she reminded me that in the highest celebration of the feminine there is no separation. Everything is connected. I especially remembered her words, "This is the hard part." Now, in the all-forgiving nature of the silence, I realized how much I made my liberal political worldview good and the conservative worldview evil. After my passionate campaigning for John Kerry, George W. Bush had been reelected as president and I had been devastated and depressed. I felt utterly separated from half of America. My dream showed me how split I felt when I made things good and evil. But now I noticed the real genius of my dream. It was a sliding screen, it was not at all an immovable wall. It was simply up to me to insist on sliding it back, just as I had done in my dream.

It was there, sitting on a bright green spot of clover that marked "the border" between two countries, that I realized if I was to grow I had to take back the "other" in my own country. I started to cry. I didn't want to do this. I didn't have a clue how to do this. I could embrace all colors, genders, sexual orientations, faiths, and cultures. But please Goddess, not the conservatives. Startled, I realized this "other" went back much further than the current conservative trend in American politics. It went back to my childhood in Wilmington, Delaware, and the way that high society had smothered my mother's free spirit and made me feel like an outsider. The continuity of my separation awed me.

As a child's courage inspires a parent to grow, so did the courage of students like Nassrin and Edward, and Rene and Michaela, inspire my next steps as a spiritual mother. I have learned so much from my students and their precious stories as they continue to move me to become all I can. How is it that I am granted the privilege of holding my individual heart so close to the universal heart of the human condition? I can only believe it is my capacity to listen well. I try to listen as if I am hearing each person's story as the very first story I have ever heard, as if the blueprint for their healing is contained in the very story they are telling. And if I listen carefully enough I can find the exact question that will open the door into their imagination. "True listening is worship," said Heidegger.

It is worship because this kind of listening demands that I empty myself. I must empty myself of the need to do something, to know the "right" answer, to fix, resolve, or control the outcome of this miraculous unfolding called a life. In this vast empty space resides an implicit trust that a person can find their way, a trust that understands a person wants the truth even more than they want to avoid pain. A faith that no matter what horror a person might be passing through, eventually they will find the answer because their imagination is stronger and brighter than any dark night of the soul. This is a mother's tender trust, a mother's fierce faith.

Here in this holy listening, this trust in the divinity of the imagination, this radical courage to stay present to pain, were the very qualities my mother had embodied when I was a young girl. Now, I had finally taken back my mother's innate emotional intelligence, her rich spirituality and vibrant intuition. They had become the very backbone of my own spiritual mothering. My mother's individual abandonment had mirrored the universal loss of the feminine. And I had traveled the globe embracing the universal in order to come back to my own particular feminine.

Now, each time I encourage a student to go fearlessly towards their pain or to appreciate the dual nature of our human predicament; each time I help someone to protect their inner life or to find their God in a nondogmatic way; and each time I insist that the highest celebration of the sacred is its inclusive embrace of all traditions and all kinds of people—I know the feminine is no longer lost to me. I know I have turned some powerful force back on itself and redeemed my mother's loss. I know I am in the house of the Great Mother.

Completing the Circle
Death as Holy Advisor

The Last Invocation

At the last, tenderly,
From the walls of the powerful fortress'd house,
From the clasp of the knitted locks, from the
    keep of the well-closed doors,
Let me be wafted.

Let me glide noiselessly forth;
With the key of softness unlock the locks-with
    a whisper,
Set open the doors O soul.

Tenderly-be not impatient,
(Strong is your hold O mortal flesh,
Strong is your hold O love.)
                                        —Walt Whitman

It is May back in the Hudson Valley, and our Benedictine
monastery is full of the scents of lilac and honeysuckle. At the
end of the driveway fluttering in the breeze like small prayer
flags, the rows of tissue paper poppies are such an audacious

orange that we almost forget that the hillside was blanketed in a foot of snow the last time this group was here. Throughout this silent retreat day we have been reveling in spring's exuberance: walking meditation outside on the cloister walk accompanied by the chant of bird song; sitting with favorite poetry books in the generous green shade of the giant trees that slope down the hill to the Hudson River; and, for a brave few, dipping in the icy river as a spring purification ritual.

Suddenly, I must leave my spot under the maple tree where I have been held spellbound by Pablo Neruda's poems. I have been summoned to the monastery guesthouse office, where my friend Brother Bede hands me a note with a telephone message. The small white piece of paper tells me that my student Francine has been killed crossing a street in New York City. Then there is a number to call for further details. The unexpected punch of sudden death wallops me in the stomach as I fall into the nearest chair. My heart is racing and I am blazing hot. I feel the slow thickness of death take her place next to the astounding vitality outside the window. I slow my breathing and then I call the number.

Elegant foxy lady in her Audi TT roadster, passionate scuba diver, visionary mentor to young people, Francine died instantly when a car hit her as she crossed an intersection in Manhattan. Francine and I were born just months apart. She died at the same age as Mom did and left a son very near the age I was when my mother died. The inevitable questions that come with sudden death crowd in on me. How can I go on with the ordinary details of the day when I have heard something like this? How and when do I tell my students, some of whom are close friends of Francine? How can it be that everything around me feels simultaneously exactly the same and totally different?

Returning to the chapel, I lead the next rounds of sitting and walking meditation. Today we are walking with the phrase

"I am here, I am here, in the now, in the now." Intoned over and over as we walk, the phrase calms me and guides me. I decide to complete the day of silence and break the news about Francine's death that evening after we share poetry, our customary way of ending a silent retreat day.

As we gather at dusk, the stately monastery room is soft with our silence and filled with the acute awareness that comes from a full day of meditation. Over the years death has often visited us in this room with the passing of grandparents, mothers and fathers, and members of our Grace community who have died of AIDS and cancer. Together we have explored the theme of death, hoping to grasp that we have daily chances to practice dying whenever we surrender to our resistances. With the plaster used in setting broken bones, we have cast stark white death masks on our living flesh to remind us that we die the way we live. Celebrating *el dia de los muertos*, we have built colorful altars spread with dozens of tiny votive candles, traditional sweets, and photos of those beloveds whom we have lost. Now, comforted by the gentle dusk and the memory of a splendid spring day, we would like to think that we understand death. But, then, each new death requires us to kneel at its feet and start over.

After poetry provides the trusted bridge from silence back into spoken word, I share the news of Francine's passing. Shock, tears, and confusion are followed by stories about Francine's vibrant life. Memorials are planned. As the evening ends we enter the monastery's Great Silence, which continues until we meet again after breakfast. Each of us must now face our loss in quiet solitude.

In my tiny monastery room with my rosaries in hand, I toss and turn in my bed. Did I handle the evening well? Did I act the way a spiritual mother should act when someone dies? Adding insult to injury, I berate myself for such a preposterous question. Then, as is so often the case when someone dies, Francine's presence offers me the very comfort I need. I remember how grateful she had been for my mentorship and how generous she had always been in thanking me during our twelve-year relationship. Traveling between fitful sleep and dreaming, my psyche visits those who have initiated me in the mysteries of dying. Standing as guardians at the gates of death, Mom and Pop appear young and dashing, as in their honeymoon pictures. Then I pass into what feels like endless space where I see thirty-year-old Gale Warner, who looks like a young girl to me now. My dear friend Peter, who was a brother to me, is asking about the spiritual retreats for gay men that we were designing when he died from AIDS at forty-four. Looking as vital as the last time I saw him, Danaan appears before he died from a sudden massive heart attack on his way to Vietnam, where for years he had been removing landmines from fields he had fought in as a young soldier. Sitting together in some kind of heavenly bleachers are all the brave people I came to know as a hospice volunteer. And finally Maud is there, her shock of white hair appearing as a luminous halo now.

That night, though I had no idea, Francine was taking her place next to those who schooled me in dying. Francine became the gatekeeper to a year when death was my constant advisor, a year where the angel of death rode on my shoulder as if she had absolutely no place else to go. Riding just above my head with her lips right next to my ear, the dark angel could be sure I listened well. Astride me in her comfortable seat she turned the seasons as the hot summer brought the suicide of the twenty-one-year-old daughter of one my students. In the autumn as the leaves began to fall, my dear friend Elizabeth Rose was diagnosed with terminal cancer and told to put her affairs in order.

I spoke with Elizabeth every few days as she fought her battles, as she became a skeleton who looked like she had survived the Holocaust, and as she told me she wanted to live past fifty-three so she could write more books. David and I were on retreat in the Caribbean when Elizabeth Rose died just after the winter solstice. We consecrated a great outcropping of red clay boulders with the turquoise sea crashing against them as an altar to our Pisces friend, a gifted astrologer. In the days following her death we took shells, magenta bougainvillea, and prayers to Rosie's chapel by the sea. One of those days, as we swam in the healing waters of the Caribbean, several continents away an immense tsunami swept though the Indian Ocean and scooped up the lives of hundreds of thousands of people. The *Times* of India described the tsunami like this: "Such stupendous forces beyond conception can only inspire awe—and ultimate humiliation in the face of a mysterious creation which, to make itself complete, must inevitably contain the seeds of its own dissolution." I felt certain the dark angel on my shoulder would have put it no differently.

We returned home to our mountain valley to one of the coldest Januarys on record, with eighteen inches of snow and temperatures resting below zero for weeks on end. The world was frozen in shock as the number of dead in Thailand, India, and Indonesia continued to rise and baffle the imagination. From our work during the Earth Run, David and I knew scores of people in the area hit by the tsunami and we wondered who had been taken. I couldn't separate Elizabeth's death from the thousands as I built a small altar on an atlas of the Indian Ocean and placed Rosie's picture there along with candles and shells. The presence on my shoulder shoves my face into questions and doubts. What does one death mean in the midst of so many? Only you, an American, has such an indulgent privilege as to spend your days writing about one precious death that took place more than thirty years ago.

January's white landscape is hauntingly beautiful, with strong winds blowing across the Ashokan Reservoir, shaping the snowdrifts into a winter sculpture garden. Near my white

Capricorn birthday I schedule an appointment with my doctor to tell him that my heart is racing too fast, seeming to never slow to its normal pace. To tell him that I am afraid I am going to die. In his book *Grief Observed*, C. S. Lewis says that grief feels so much like fear, like the worst kind of anxiety. Knowing my family medical history and that I have just lost Elizabeth, Dr. Mike reminds me of the other times when I have faced loss and felt certain that I was going to die. Though Dr. Mike is a wry and mystical kind of guy, I don't tell him that this time the dark angel is right there on my shoulder and that maybe, as a doctor, he could make it leave. Checking my heart he decides that it is, in fact, beating too fast. Just to be safe, he assures me, we'll do an echocardiogram and order a halter that will carefully monitor my heart for twenty-four hours. It's probably just tachycardia, he adds.

There's another blizzard the day that I go to the hospital to get the small halter monitor with wires taped all over my chest. Driving home from the hospital, the snow blurs with images of my mother in intensive care after her open-heart surgery. Although I am certain the results will prove my impending death, the diagnosis is tachycardia most likely brought on by my menopause.

More snow, more rapid heartbeats, and more death. A member of my close community in Woodstock loses her sister to cancer. E-mails bring news from various students whose parents have died. My work begins to put me in close contact with women from Kosovo, Afghanistan, and Rwanda who have witnessed the unspeakable atrocities of war and genocide. David and I initiate proposals and fundraising plans to use our empowerment model in their reconciliation work. Hearing their stories, again I struggle with the question of the relevance of one death when these women have lost their entire families or even their entire villages. And another woman considers herself lucky even though she has been repeatedly raped, because she's still alive and plenty of the women she knows are dead. Dead in the most ungodly ways you can possibly imagine.

Nonetheless, as the red buds of April arrive, I am finishing up this book about the influence of one death on my life. As I write, the weeks pass and soon splashes of yellow forsythia spill over the mountains announcing early May. Almost a year since Francine died, almost four years since I began work on this book. The day I am finally ready to complete the manuscript I find myself uncharacteristically weeping. Coming into my office David finds me in tears. "Gailee, what's wrong? You should be celebrating, you are completing such a long, arduous process." He strokes my head tenderly.

"I know," I say blowing my nose. "The writing was so cathartic and such a wonderful way to spend time with my mother. Now that it's almost over I guess I am going to miss Mom."

"Can I get you some tea or anything?" As he has done now for twenty-five years, my husband asks what I need.

"Sure, that would be great. I think I'll just print out the manuscript tomorrow," I say wearily. "I need to finish my thoughts for Elizabeth's memorial this weekend. I thought I would use several of Walt Whitman's short poems on death as the closing prayer. Remember, sweetie, we have to leave at noon on Saturday."

Just hours later as I was finishing what I would say at our friend's service, David came back into my office, ashen. Taking my hand, his voice shaking, David tells me, "Gail, your brother Jimmy has just died from a massive heart attack while playing basketball." A wail escapes from deep within my gut, a primitive sound that I have never made before. Again, like just a year ago, my heart is racing and I am blazing hot. Again, I feel the thickness of death take her place next to the brilliant yellow forsythia outside my window. My constant companion these four seasons, now the dark angel enfolds me in a cloak so thick and so coarse I feel nothing else.

My brother's memorial is two days after Elizabeth's and I will be invoking Walt Whitman's poems more than once. The day after Jimmy's service I am to lead a Grace retreat for fifty-five students. I am completely overwhelmed. Desperate for support I e-mail my Woodstock community and my Helix Sisters telling them that I am lost and overwhelmed. I ask them to pray for Jimmy and his family and to say this prayer for me, "Gail, may you be strong, may you stay soft and in touch with your feelings. May you know that you are held in the arms of God." My dear friends, the brothers at the monastery, say a mass for Jimmy and prayers for me and for my family. Soon hundreds of my students learn of my shock and the prayers I have requested. Gradually, the thick, coarse cloak of death is replaced by the spacious comforting cloak of prayer—that comforting cloak that Mom had first taught me about as a young girl sitting next to her at mass.

Deciding to honor my brother as if my mother and father were speaking about him, I prepared my remarks for Jimmy's service. I hope that since I have cried so much as I wrote the words that this somehow ensures that I won't break down as I deliver them. Having just completed my manuscript, my life is already in bas-relief as I drive back to my childhood in Wilmington. Arriving at Tower Hill, where they have closed the school for my brother's memorial, his students have made and pasted a thousand origami peace cranes all over Jimmy's classroom. Seven hundred people crowd the packed auditorium: teachers who taught with my father and who taught me; classmates of mine who now chair the most prestigious boards of directors in Wilmington, including the Tower Hill School; students who adore my brother and handsome young men who were coached and mentored by him over the years.

As I offer the tribute to my brother, my entire childhood in Wilmington passes before me. Speaking from Pop's voice, I say how proud he would have been that Jimmy followed in his footsteps at Tower Hill and that he was such an outstanding role model to his two sons. Once again I feel how my father made a good life in Wilmington. Speaking from Mom's voice I say how proud she would have been of my brother's tender heart, his steadfastness as a husband and a father, sheltering his family from the storms of life. Once again I cannot help but feel that my mother's dreams were not fulfilled. In the two-hour receiving line after the service just about everyone who had known my mother exclaimed, "Gail, you look just like Jacquie!" I wanted to ask them, "Is the resemblance because I have tried to live the life my mother never had? Is it because I have spent the past three years finally getting to know my mother?"

Later that evening Joanie and I went back to our bed and breakfast in the Brandywine River Valley just ten minutes from our childhood home. Passing Brecks Lane and St. Joseph's Church, the Pancake Run and the Bubble and Squeak Railroad, we reminisced about our inseparable days as young tomboys. We had remained close while Jimmy had made his life separate from ours in the place that both Joanie and I had needed to leave. Jimmy took his place next to Pop; Joanie and I took paths our mother might have been glad to follow. Later, lying in bed and musing about my family, I thought about the radically different responses my brother and sister had offered me when I had asked them to e-mail me their overall impressions of our mother in order to help me write this book. Jimmy remembered Mom as the happiest person he had ever met, and most of Joanie's memories were of our mother's anger, both toward her and life in general. Like most siblings, we reflected different aspects of our mother; Jimmy held her joy, Joanie carried her anger, and I adopted Mom's sadness and heartbreak. Each of these reflections was an equally true part of our mother.

Fluffing up my pillows and trying to sleep, I was awed at how mysterious and subjective all memory is. Surely my mother, my father, and my brother were each a rich and contrasting composite of all the memories of all the people who knew them. Surely, memory is just as much about the person doing the remembering as the one remembered.

Finally falling asleep that night in the green valley where I had grown up, I realized that my brother's death completed the circle of grieving for my mother. My visceral response to Jimmy's death, with my willingness to go toward it and to ask for support, showed that I had reversed my long solitary denial about Mom's death, and about all death. Then, I gently lifted the dark angel sitting on my shoulder and placed her in front of me. I looked her softly in the eyes and said, "I welcome you as my holy advisor. Finally, I see that you have been teaching me for a long time. You started with Pop's deeply repressed, unspoken response to his father's suicide, which seeped into every aspect of my life. You were informing me when Mom died so young and I ran from this for so many years. Placing me in contact with women all over the world who have experienced war and genocide, you have blessed me. By asking me to face an unusual number of early deaths with Gale, Peter, Francine, Elizabeth, and now my brother, Jimmy, you have mentored me. And you have demanded that I face my own fear of dying. Finally I can say to you, I am grateful for all of this."

Then, as I talked woman to woman with Lady Death, I felt my mother's presence. I saw more clearly than ever how gracefully Mom had lived with death as her close advisor. Though she had betrayed many aspects of her feminine wisdom, she had never abandoned her acute respect for death, thus paying one of the highest tributes to the sacred feminine. Indeed, it was precisely my mother's respect for death that allowed her to let me go and live so fully even as she faced her own dying. Who else but the Great Mother would insist that I understand that life and death are two halves of the same whole? And who else but the Great Mother would insist that I recognize that over the course of writing honestly about Mom's death, I had become willing to face many deaths? And then I knew for sure that it was my mother who had sent the dark angel to sit on my shoulder this entire past year, this year as I was finishing my tribute to her.

Some days after returning home from Jimmy's funeral I take out my mother's battered old army green painter's box, the one she would often bring out for the imaginative adventures of my childhood. Of all my mother's possessions this is the one I treasure the most. Lifting the lid, there I find her brushes, pens, oil paints, charcoals, and inks. Even then her scent was still mingled with the smell of the paint. I cannot open this box without weeping, without pressing my face into its contents to bring back her memory. I cannot open it without saying to her how sorry I am that she didn't get to fulfill her creative dreams. I cannot open it without saying, "I have done my best to fulfill my own dreams partly as an antidote to your unfulfillment, and, yes, partly because this is the life I chose." And now I can also say to her that in writing this story about us, I have found my true voice as a writer. This voice is not just hers and mine, it is also the voice of all those who long to take back the wisdom of the feminine.

That night I had a vivid dream about my mother. She rarely appears in my dreams any more so I knew this was special. The dream opens with the fragrance of my mother's scent mingled with the smell of her paints. Then I see Mom is trying to find me at JFK Airport in New York. She is frantically looking for me. Around and around she circles the airport. She can't find me anywhere. Suddenly I remember I haven't told her the flight or the airline that I will arrive on. She has none of the information she needs to find me. I awake in a cold sweat.

How perfect that Mom is looking for me at Kennedy Airport. The last time I saw my mother healthy was when she and my father dropped me off at JFK for my Peace Corps service. Then I returned there twice more during her lifetime, once for her open-heart surgery and then for her funeral. My mother and I never really had time to find each other while she was alive. Yet here she is in my dreamscape, the holiest of the invisible realms of the feminine, still trying to find me in one of the final places we were together. In Colette's book *My Mother's House*, she wrote, "The personage of my mother . . . haunts me still . . . I am not sure I have discovered all she bequeathed . . . to me. I have come to this task late."

But it's never too late.

Acknowledgments

To Ned Leavitt for staying with me during the long arduous birth of this book, I am deeply grateful. For my editors Caroline Pincus and Nan Satter, I am blessed beyond measure to have you both as mentors. Greta Sibley, this book has come to life through your design artistry and grace. Rachel Hockett and Gretchen Gordon, for your meticulous attention. Jeff DeRose, for your sensitive photography used on the cover. Margo Baldwin and Peg O'Donnell, I am so proud to be part of the Chelsea Green Publishing family, where you uphold so many of the values I believe in.

Chris Northrup, your support of this book has meant more to me than words can convey. Your heartfelt encouragement kept me going when I was almost ready to give up. To my dear sister, Joanie McLean, for supporting this book even though you had a very different relationship with our mother, and most important, for our ever-deepening sisterhood. For my beloved assistant Laura Peeling, thank you for your impeccability and for basically being an angel come down to earth.

Thank you to dear friends and colleagues who read different portions of the manuscript and offered support and guidance: Elizabeth Lesser, Margit Colagrande, Cheryl Richardson, Susan Richards, Nancy Evans, Gunilla Norris, Ellen Wingard, Ro King, Danit Fried, Loung Ung, Kali Rosenblum, and Carla Goldstein.

For all my students all over the world who have taught me how to be a spiritual mother, I love you and I bow to you.

Finally to my husband David Gershon; without your support I could not have brought this book into the world. You are the love of my life, my closest colleague, and a great inspiration. I am grateful for all we have learned from each other about balancing masculine and feminine wisdom.